Augmenting Customer Experience with SharePoint Online

Building Portals and Practices to Improve Usability

Charles Waghmare

Apress®

Augmenting Customer Experience with SharePoint Online: Building Portals and Practices to Improve Usability

Charles Waghmare
Mumbai, India

ISBN-13 (pbk): 978-1-4842-5533-9 ISBN-13 (electronic): 978-1-4842-5534-6
https://doi.org/10.1007/978-1-4842-5534-6

Managing Director, Apress Media LLC: Welmoed Spahr
Acquisitions Editor: Smriti Srivastava
Development Editor: Matthew Moodie
Coordinating Editor: Shrikant Vishwakarma

Cover designed by eStudioCalamar

Cover image designed by Freepik (www.freepik.com)

Distributed to the book trade worldwide by Springer Science+Business Media New York, 233 Spring Street, 6th Floor, New York, NY 10013. Phone 1-800-SPRINGER, fax (201) 348-4505, e-mail orders-ny@springer-sbm.com, or visit www.springeronline.com. Apress Media, LLC is a California LLC and the sole member (owner) is Springer Science + Business Media Finance Inc (SSBM Finance Inc). SSBM Finance Inc is a **Delaware** corporation.

For information on translations, please e-mail rights@apress.com, or visit http://www.apress.com/rights-permissions.

Apress titles may be purchased in bulk for academic, corporate, or promotional use. eBook versions and licenses are also available for most titles. For more information, reference our Print and eBook Bulk Sales web page at http://www.apress.com/bulk-sales.

Any source code or other supplementary material referenced by the author in this book is available to readers on GitHub via the book's product page, located at www.apress.com/978-1-4842-5533-9. For more detailed information, please visit http://www.apress.com/source-code.

Printed on acid-free paper

God is our refuge and strength,
an ever-present help in trouble.
Therefore, we will not fear, though the earth give way
and the mountains fall into the heart of the sea,
though its waters roar and foam
and the mountains quake with their surging

—Psalm 46:1-3

In the beginning, I would offer honor and praise to my God, Lord Jesus Christ, who has been giving me opportunities to author books. I am grateful to my God, Lord Christ, and dedicate this book to Him and to His glory.

My Dedication:

My Dearest parents, my father Mr. David Genu Waghmare and my mother Mrs. Kamla Waghmare, whose love is eternal. From the bottom of my heart, I thank my parents for their care, encouragement, and motivation until this day. God bless them.

My dearest sisters, Mrs. Carol Kamble and Mrs. Mary Unhavane for their love, care, and support.

My adorable nephews: Kris – a world of gyms, fitness, and computers. Savio – a world of Harmonium, Tanpura, and classical music. Enjoy spending time with them.

Miss. Priya Muniraj, my fiancée, for her prayers, affection and care.

Table of Contents

About the Author

Charles Waghmare has been working with Shell as a Business Analyst in the area of Office 365 services such as SharePoint Online, Yammer, and Teams.

Before Shell, he was working with Capgemini since 2011 for a period of eight years, in various roles such as Yammer Community Manager, managing an Enterprise Knowledge Management platform called KM3; and developing a Knowledge Management platform for a Digital Customer Experience (DCX) organization using SharePoint Online, to manage client references and knowledge assets related to Artificial Intelligence and customer experience (CX) and promoting Microsoft Azure Chatbots to automate processes, develop proactive conversations with users, and create new use cases.

Before Capgemini, Charles worked with ATOS (formerly SIEMENS Information Systems limited) for a period of five years starting in 2011. In his tenure, he was a Community Manager of SAP-based communities where he managed communities using Technoweb 2.0 – a Yammer-like platform. In this Communities of Practice (CoP) initiative, Charles was also responsible for managing community sites built in SharePoint. Further, at ATOS, Charles was the global rollout manager for a structured document-management system built in SharePoint.

Charles loves reading motivational books, and his favorite book is *The Monk Who Sold His Ferrari.*

About the Technical Reviewer

Arun Sharma is leading Cloud business at Paytm Cloud across the regions as General Manager-Enterprise Cloud. He has vast experience on Cloud technologies (Microsoft Azure, AWS, GSuite), IoT, ML, Micro services, Bots, Docker, and Containerization. He has almost 17 years' experience in a wide variety of roles such as Delivery Manager at Microsoft, Product Manager at Icertis, Lead and Architect Associate at Infosys, Executive Trainer at Aptech, and Development Consultant at CMC. He managed relationship, sales, cloud consumption, consulting services, and adoption with medium- and large-sized global customers.

Arun loves challenges in the Microsoft playing field, combining it with his domain knowledge in Banking, Insurance, FMCG, Government (Local), Retail, and Telecom. He is very active in the community as the author of international research papers, technical speaker, reviewer, blogs, and LinkedIn Sales Navigator. He is also recognized with the title of MCT from Microsoft and also doing a Doctor of Business administration post his MBA & M. Tech. (CS). Arun Sharma can be found on Twitter at @arunkhoj.

Acknowledgments

Late Mr. Ranjan Majumdar-ex business leader at ATOS-Syntel, CGI and Manipal, for being my Eternal Inspiration (though I have never seen him).

Mr. Manish Saxena, Director, ATOS-Syntel, for his guidance.

Mrs. Shruti Udupa, Manager at Accenture, to act as a God-sent angel during my life's most difficult situation.

Miss Shilpi Prasad, Senior Manager at Capgemini, for her kind support.

The Salvation Army Church, Matunga Corps, Mumbai and Amazing Grace AG Church, Bangalore, and special thanks to all church members for their love and affection.

CHAPTER 1

Introducing SharePoint Online Features

In the last couple of decades, we have been exposed to varieties of technologies such as SMAC (social media, analytics, cloud), big data, mobile apps, enterprise search, bots, and robotic process automation (RPA). And there are methodologies such as Agile, DevOps, Lean, and Six Sigma. But due to ever-growing customer expectations, the focus has moved to augment customer experience (CX) using a combination of different technologies that include SharePoint Online. Some core identified practices to build CX are front-end UI/UX, customer management, content management and marketing, commerce and customer process, and integration.

Digital customer experience (DCX) is all about creating an awesome customer experience, and in more realistic terms it is to make a customer's life really much easier. Technology is a key enabler to create DCX and, in this book, we will explore SharePoint Online technology so that you can effective use it to create awesome customer experience. Augmenting DCX with the help of SharePoint technology is a key principle of this book. In the beginning of the book, we have dedicated the initial chapters to understand features of SharePoint Online technology and get a down-to-earth

© Charles Waghmare 2020
C. Waghmare, *Augmenting Customer Experience with SharePoint Online*,
https://doi.org/10.1007/978-1-4842-5534-6_1

understanding of DCX. In this first chapter, we will make an introduction to SharePoint Online technology, describe features of SharePoint Online, introduce SharePoint Online admin features, and finally, highlight some key features to create DCX.

SharePoint Online – An Introduction

Microsoft SharePoint Online in Office 365 allows people to share, collaborate, connect together, update and engage others across the company, transform business processes, and harness knowledge. In addition, SharePoint Online has capabilities for organizations to protect and manage data and to build custom solutions. Primarily, organizations use SharePoint Online to create intranet websites. It is very easy that in Office 365, you can create a SharePoint site from the SharePoint start page. Whenever a new SharePoint site is created, as a part of the Office 365 group, a team site also gets created.

To access SharePoint Online services, all you need is a web browser, such as Microsoft Edge, Internet Explorer, Google Chrome, or Mozilla Firefox. Also, get the SharePoint mobile app to stay connected from your mobile devices. SharePoint Online is made available on your PC, Mac, or mobile device. The SharePoint document library and SharePoint sites are the two core features of SharePoint Online.

When you sign in to Office 365, you are exposed to various Office 365 online services through an app launcher as shown in Figure 1-1. Select SharePoint Online service to explore it.

Figure 1-1. *Sign in to SharePoint Online Service*

Introduction to SharePoint Document Library

A SharePoint document library is a unique and secure place to store files where you and your team can access them easily from any device at any time. For example, you can use a document library on a SharePoint Online site to store all files related to a specific project or a specific client. In document libraries, adding files or moving them between folders is as simple as dragging and dropping them from one location to another. See Figure 1-2.

Figure 1-2. *A SharePoint document library*

In a document library, the following can happen:

- Files can be uploaded, edited, deleted, and downloaded.

- Files can be co-authored at any given moment of time.

- Permission management features are available for the document library.

- Receive a notification when a file is modified and track its activity such as when the file was last modified.

- Customize the view of the document library.

- Share files or folders with larger teams.

- Inside the document library, add a link of another document or an internal or external URL.

- Highlight a link, file, or folder in a document library so that you and others can view them quickly.

Upload Files into SharePoint Document Library

You can upload files into SharePoint Online for better collaboration among your team members and to facilitate an easy exchange of content. When you do so, you upload files into SharePoint Document Libraries. If you use Microsoft Edge as browser, you can upload either files or folders. Follow the steps to upload files into a SharePoint document library.

1. Open SharePoint site document library as seen in Figure 1-3.

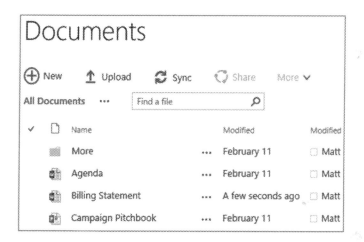

Figure 1-3. *Open SharePoint Document Library*

2. Select Upload at the top of the documents as seen in Figure 1-4.

Figure 1-4. *Select Upload at the top of the document library*

3. Once you select Upload, then you will get a
    dialog box telling you that you can select single
    or multiple files for upload. Click OK once you've
    selected your files.

Create Different SharePoint Sites

There are two choices: a team site or communication site. Let's start with a
team site.

Creating a Team Site

A SharePoint team site allows you to connect you and your team to the
organizational- or project-level content, information, and apps that
are required on a day-to-day basis. You can use a team site to store
and collaborate on files or another way is to create and manage lists
of information. On any team site home page, you can access links to
important team files, apps, and web pages and can see recent site activity
in the activity feed. See Figure 1-5.

Figure 1-5. *Example of a Team site*

To access your team site from the SharePoint start page, go the Files section of your Office 365 group if Office 365 Groups is enabled, or on the go with the SharePoint mobile apps. You can also find your SharePoint files in OneDrive (Figure 1-6).

Figure 1-6. *Mobile view of SharePoint Online through Mobile app*

A SharePoint Online team site consists of a group of related web pages, a default document library for files, lists for data management, and webparts that you can customize to meet your business needs. Let's see how we can create a team site.

1. Sign in to Office 365 and access SharePoint Online service.

2. At the top of the SharePoint page, click + Create site and choose the Team or Communication site option to create such a site. A team site creation wizard will appear on the screen where you input the information to create a team site. See Figure 1-7.

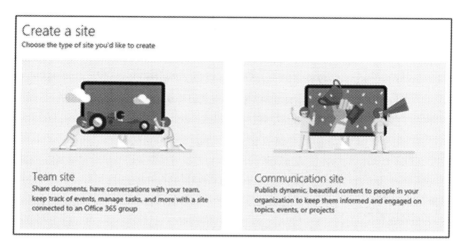

Figure 1-7. *Option to select between Team or Communication site*

3. Select the design you want to use for your site. For example, see Figure 1-8.

Figure 1-8. *Select design for your Team site*

4. Give your new team site a name, and add some text in the site description box.

5. In the Privacy settings section, choose either Public – anyone in the organization can access this site or Private – only members can access this site to control who has access to your site.

6. Choose data sensitivity for your site from options such as confidential, internal, high business impact, low business, and impact.

7. Select a language for your site and choose additional owners for your site.

8. Hit the Next button as shown in Figure 1-9, then add additional owners as shown in Figure 1-10 to complete the site creation process.

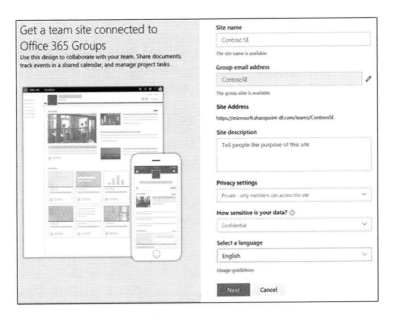

Figure 1-9. *Add Team site details*

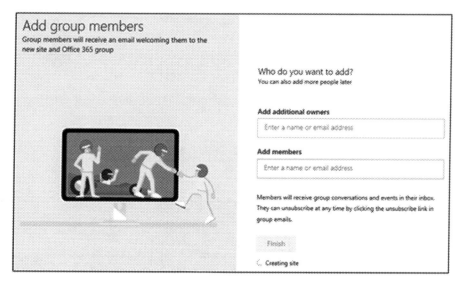

Figure 1-10. *Add additional team details to Team site*

9. Finally, add members to your site and click the
    Finish button for the site to publish (Figure 1-11).

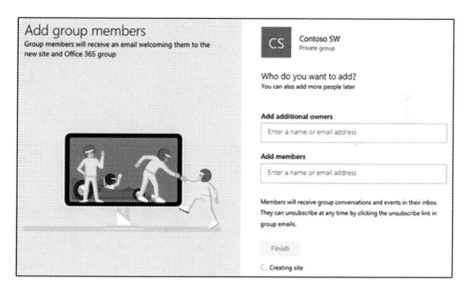

Figure 1-11. *Add owners and members*

Creating a Communication Site

A SharePoint communication site is a place to share information with others. You can share news, reports, statuses, and other information in a visually compelling format. Figure 1-12 shows a communication site in a website view.

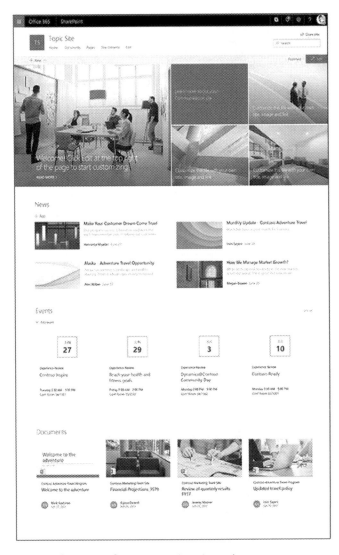

Figure 1-12. *Web view of communication site*

Figure 1-13 shows a mobile view.

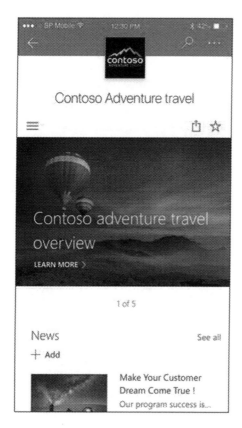

Figure 1-13. *Mobile view of Communication sites*

Below are the steps to create SharePoint communication sites. The steps are simple and easy to understand.

1. Sign in to Office 365.

2. From the app launcher available on the top left, choose SharePoint tile.

3. After selection, at the top of the SharePoint
    home page, you will see an option to create a
    site as seen in Figure 1-14, and choose the create
    communication site option as seen in Figure 1-15.

Figure 1-14. *Option to create SharePoint site*

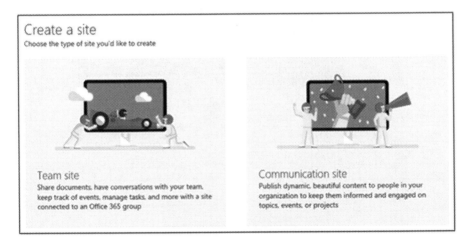

Figure 1-15. *Create Communication site*

4. Select one of the following site designs:

    •   Topic design to share information such as news,
        events, and other content.

    •   Showcase design to use photos or images to
        showcase a product, team, or event.

    •   Blank design to create your own design.

Figure 1-16 is the user interface where you can choose your design.

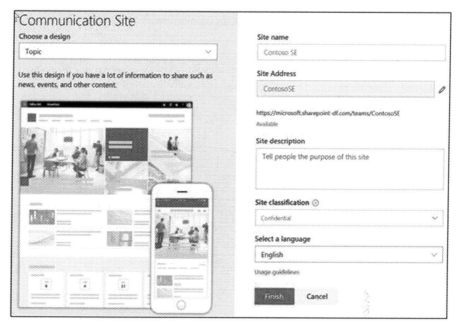

Figure 1-16. *Update Communication site details*

Explore SharePoint Hub Sites

The objective of hub sites is to bring together various components of organizational intranet under one single place. They can also be referred as a set of steps as one can adopt it to create a successful intranet. Hub sites are popularly known as "connective tissue," which aims to tie a collection of team sites and communications sites into one strong unit. One prime aspect of creating digital intranets or social intranets based on SharePoint Online is that different components of the intranet ideally should be built as a different site collection; that is, there could be a communication site or team site so that each site can manage content and its permissions appropriately to have updated information available for the user community. A hub site (very commonly created from a communication site on SharePoint Online) can be considered as an umbrella of different components of an intranet that attempts to bring different communication and team sites together.

Team and communication sites can be hub sites. Besides these, you can create a traditional site collection in a classic experience to manage your content (Figure 1-17).

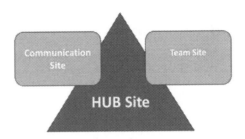

Figure 1-17. *SharePoint Online Modern Sites*

SharePoint Online Features

In this section of the chapter, we will look at some of the SharePoint Online features as well as explore SharePoint Online admin features as well. Following are some widely used SharePoint Online features:

File Storage: Provides options to upload, store, and share files.

External Sharing: Share attachments or files with your suppliers, partners, and clients who are outside your organization.

Content Management: Manage and organize content with metadata, records management, and retention policy.

Team Sites: A dedicated place for your team to collaborate and share documents, news, and information to stay updated.

Communication Sites: Broadly communicate your message across your organization by publishing beautiful content to keep them informed and engaged on topics, events, or projects.

Intranets: With this feature, you would be able to share exciting client stories, leadership views and opinions, new deals, organizational charts, and what's happening in your organization.

Mobile Apps: With this feature you can access your content just from anywhere in the world and without any time restrictions.

Automate work: With this feature, one can set up alerts and workflows to automate processes.

Discovery: With this feature, one is able to discover very valuable content and people when required to do so.

Search: With this feature, one will be able to search content and find what is expected in the search results.

E-Discovery: With this feature, one can discover content in an electronic format for legal and audit purposes.

Data loss prevention capabilities (DLP): Use of advanced DLP capabilities to monitor data loss and information security protection.

In-Place Hold: Prevent content from editing and deleting.

SharePoint Online Admin

Global administrators in Office 365 have rights to assign users with SharePoint administrator roles to manage SharePoint Online admin features. Global admin by default exists as a SharePoint admin. When you decide to purchase a Microsoft 365 or Office 365 subscription, a default team site is automatically created, and the global admin gets configured as the primary site collection administrator. When you assign a SharePoint admin role, you can assign the role of Service administrator in order to see important information in the Microsoft 365 admin center, such as the health of the SharePoint Online service, as well as change and release notifications (Figure 1-18).

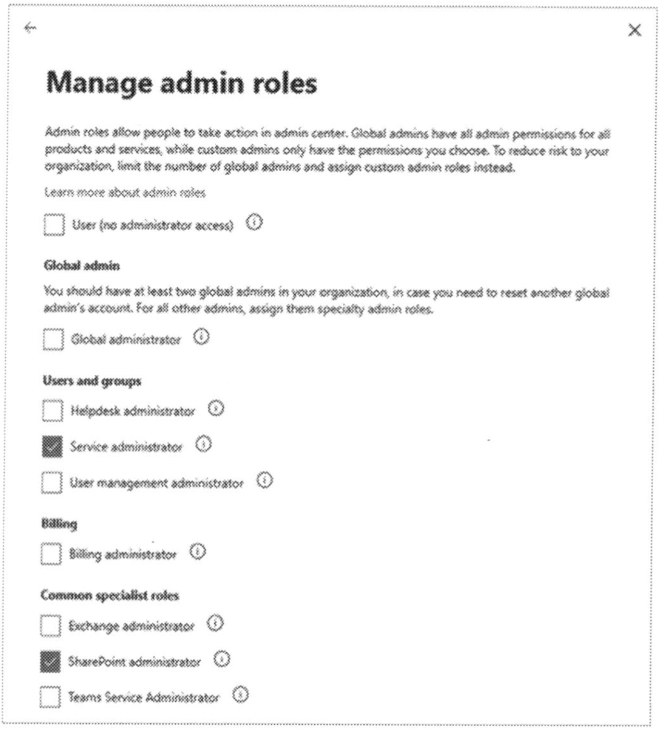

Figure 1-18. Assign service admin to role to SharePoint admin

Users with a SharePoint admin role are able to access the SharePoint admin center and have options to create and manage site collections, designate site collection administrators, manage user profiles, and more. In addition, SharePoint admins can now manage Office 365 groups, including creating, deleting, and restoring groups, as well as changing group owners.

Site admins are a group of users that have permission to manage sites (previously called "site collections"), including the site root and any subsites. They don't need to have an admin role in Office 365 and cannot access the SharePoint admin center. A SharePoint site can have several site administrators but must have one and only one primary administrator. Below are some key tasks of the SharePoint administrator:

- Create sites

- Delete sites

- Manage site collections and global settings

- Turn external sharing on or off for SharePoint Online

- Add and remove site admins

- Manage site collection storage limits

- Manage SharePoint Online user profiles

SharePoint Online DCX Features

In this last section of the chapter, we will look at some key features of SharePoint Online that will help to build DCX. In subsequent chapters, we will take a deep-dive look into DCX.

We will take a brief look at the out-of-the-box webparts of the SharePoint communication and team sites, which help to design visually appealing SharePoint communication and team sites and thus create great DCX. Customers want to find information easily, communicate simply between users, and finally, there is definitely business value for end users to reuse information. Let's explore some elements of SharePoint communication and team sites to create an awesome user experience.

Webparts

In this section we will discover webparts available under topic, showcase, and blank categories that are available in the communication and team site templates:

Topic:

- **Events** – Publish upcoming organizational and engagement events.

- **Highlighted content** – Distinguish specific content from other content by applying filters.

- **Hero** – Generate visual and focus interest to your SharePoint site.

- **News** – Create and publish eye-catching news, announcements, and updates.

Showcase:

- **Hero** – Generate visual and focus interest to your SharePoint site.

- **Image Gallery** – Insert image or collection of images into Team or Communication sites.

Blank:

- Add maps in pages using Bing maps.

- Embed content from other sites using an Embed webpart.

- Insert files such as Excel, PowerPoint, and PDFs in your pages using File viewer.

- Receive alerts and messages based on a condition you set using Connectors.

- Managing files, that is, to upload, download, and modify onsite using a Document library.

- Insert Office 365 Group Calendar using Group Calendar.

- Break line between webparts using Divider.

- Add a link to external and internal page using Link.

- Create an instant preview to share a preview of Kindle book using Kindle.

- Select people for contact purposes using People to add.

- Set up team actions in your page using Planner.

- Embed report created in Power BI.

- Add customized apps built by themselves using PowerApps.

- Use a video to display video in your communication sites using Office 365.

- Create surveys, quizzes, and polls using Microsoft forms.

- Add simple charts in your page using Quick Chart.

- Create a collaborative experience for your end user using Yammer.

- Add paragraphs, tables, styles, bullets, indentations, highlights, and hyperlinks using Text.

- Display tweets linked to your organization and its interests using Twitter.

- Display the current weather on your page using Weather.

- Using Site, showcase sites on a page to automatically show sites associated to the hub site.

- Control vertical space on your page using Spacer.

- Display a video from the Microsoft stream using Stream.

- Pin items to your page for easy access using Quick links.

- Display recent activity on your communication site using Site Activity.

Mobile

SharePoint Online for communication and team sites can be accessed through a mobile app. Organizations are sometimes reluctant to invest in a mobile app with a perception that it is just an internal company site. SharePoint Online offers mobile access, which means sites are digitally transformed to access them through a mobile app. With smartphones, engaging users through mobile devices has become simple. SharePoint communication sites provide a simple way to consume and create content on the go using mobile devices. A mobile app helps to view pages, navigate, search, create articles, and engage in Yammer conversations. The SharePoint mobile app is available for Android, Windows Phone, and iPhone.

Collaborative

Yammer facilitates collaboration and offers the option to add feeds in the communication or team site from specific Yammer groups. The objective to create digital content management systems such as SharePoint Online are designed in such a way that its consumers should not only read and view content but should be in a position to react over content, share it further, and comment over it. Brainstorming and generating new ideas to create content for an intranet can be possible through Yammer engagement.

Customization

SharePoint Online communication and team sites offer plenty of options for customization such as edit or change logo, create customized theme to match with company brand, add useful links, edit pages, and add webparts. Some companies have created sports competition campaigns on their intranet built using communication sites, by setting a daily quiz and winners.

Communication or team sites are customized by some organizations with a smart engine called an integrated search engine that offers search results across all platforms. This is achieved by providing a UI of a search engine on the intranet home page. Organizations, in order to gain maximum viewers, are thinking of adding features such as book Uber rides; embed feeds of external social media channels such as Facebook, LinkedIn, and Instagram; and shopping sites for employees to make purchases and embed feeds linked to the company.

Summary

With this, we have come to the end of this chapter where we have introduced SharePoint Online technology, described features of SharePoint Online, introduced SharePoint Online admin features, and finally, highlighted some key features to create DCX. In the following chapter, we will explore top SharePoint Online features so that a user can jumpstart their digital transformation journey. There are features to change the look and feel, deep dive into out-of-the-box webparts, and features to create team collaboration and SharePoint Online themes.

CHAPTER 2

Office 365 and SharePoint Online for a DCX

In the previous chapter, we explored features of SharePoint Online, introduced a few SharePoint online admin features, and highlighted some key features to create a digital customer experience. In this chapter, we will explore the Office 365 product family and top SharePoint Online webparts in detail, which will help us to create a digital customer experience. This exploration will help us to design and modify the look and feel of SharePoint sites, the effective use of out-of-the-box webparts, and configure collaborative spaces and report usage reports. In the beginning we will take a deep dive into the Office 365 product family, as it will help to create a digital customer experience along with SharePoint Online through seamless integration, which is available in default.

© Charles Waghmare 2020
C. Waghmare, *Augmenting Customer Experience with SharePoint Online*,
https://doi.org/10.1007/978-1-4842-5534-6_2

Office 365 – An Introduction

Microsoft Office 365 is a subscription service that offers productivity tools to execute work done in the modern enterprise. Productivity tools are not confined to Office suite such as Word, Excel, and Email; but there are collaborative tools such TEAMS, Yammer, and OneNote, which help people to effectively connect, collaborate, and share during the execution of work. Further, seamless integration of these tools makes accessibility very easy with smooth sharing of content from one tool to another. The Office 365 product family is available in the form of a subscription; therefore, organizations do not have to worry about hosting, maintaining, and upgrading. Office 365 is available in the form SaaS – Software-as-a-Service, that is, you pay for usage only, and Microsoft will take of managing these other tools. See Figure 2-1.

Figure 2-1. *Office 365 Product Family*

Office 365 contains varieties of tools such as Office, Sway, Yammer, TEAMS, and others. Let's try to understand these tools in detail, which will help us to adopt them to create digital customer experiences. All Office 365 apps have a common navigation bar, sometimes called Office 365 tiles, as shown in Figure 2-2.

Figure 2-2. *Navigating Office 365 apps*

In the Office 365 product family, different types of tools exist such as Content creation, Content hosting, and employee collaboration and communication. Also, there are a few tools that can be used to build applications. For content creation, Office apps such as Word, PowerPoint, Excel, and OneNote are used. For hosting content there are OneDrive, SharePoint, and Stream. For employee collaboration and communication, Yammer TEAMS, Sway, Outlook, and Forms exist. To build applications, there are power apps, flow, Planner, Tasks, and Calendar; People are used more from a Project Management standpoint. Power BI is used for reporting purposes, Delve for search, and Dynamics for Customer Relationship Management. Let's explore widely used popular tools.

- **OneNote**: It is an efficient tool to capture notes in the form text, drawing, or by adding images. Further, OneNote allows you to organize and reuse your notes across all your devices. See Figure 2-3.

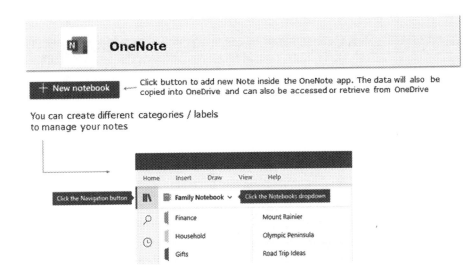

Figure 2-3. OneNote

- **OneDrive**: Microsoft provides up to 1 TB of cloud storage in OneDrive for Business. It is very similar to the "My Document" folder, which is normally preferred for storing attachments locally. See Figure 2-4.

Figure 2-4. *OneDrive for Business*

- **Delve**: Delve manages the Office 365 profile to discover and organize information to be most interesting across Office 365. You will only see documents that you already have access to. Other people will not see your private documents (Figure 2-5). With Delve you can do the following:

Figure 2-5. *Discover information using Delve*

- Connect and collaborate organization wide,

- Search for people and documents (Figure 2-6),

Figure 2-6. *Search People or information using Delve*

- Access work-in-progress documents and learn more about them,

- With Delve, discover and organize information across Office 365,

- Stay connected and productive wherever you are.

- **Microsoft Forms** allows you to quickly and easily create custom quizzes, surveys, questionnaires, registrations, and more (Figure 2-7).

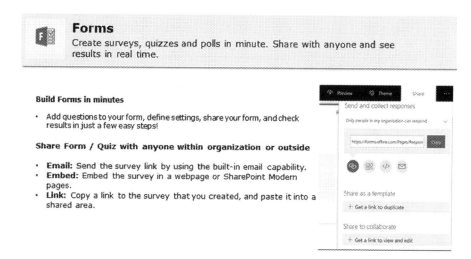

Forms

Create surveys, quizzes and polls in minute. Share with anyone and see results in real time.

Build Forms in minutes

- Add questions to your form, define settings, share your form, and check results in just a few easy steps!

Share Form / Quiz with anyone within organization or outside

- **Email:** Send the survey link by using the built-in email capability.
- **Embed:** Embed the survey in a webpage or SharePoint Modern pages.
- **Link:** Copy a link to the survey that you created, and paste it into a shared area.

Figure 2-7. *Microsoft Forms*

- **Microsoft Stream**: View organizational videos in the Stream application or in other applications you use every day—any time, on any device (Figure 2-8).

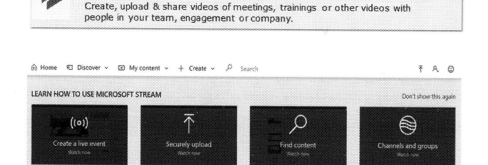

Stream

Create, upload & share videos of meetings, trainings or other videos with people in your team, engagement or company.

Figure 2-8. *Microsoft Stream*

- **Sway:** Create newsletters, presentations, and communications using Sway (Figure 2-9).

31

Sway

Create and share engaging interactive reports, presentations, stories and more

Start Creating
Create a new Sway from scratch, from content in an existing file or from a Topic

- On the **Welcome to Sway** page, choose:
  - **Create New** - to start from scratch.
  - **Start from a topic** - to have Sway provide a base content for you. Type your topic in the **Enter a topic** box, and then select **Create outline**.
- **Start from a document** - to import content from an existing file. Select the file, and then select **Open**.

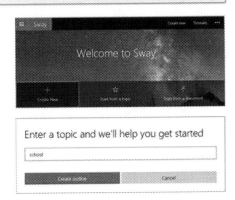

Figure 2-9. Sway

- **Teams**: It is a collaborative platform designed for project-specific collaboration. Besides, Teams has an audio and video conference facility very similar with Skype for business (Figure 2-10).

Teams

Customizable Chat - based team workspace

With Microsoft Teams
- Build a team.
- Use chat over email.
- Multiple edit of files at same instance
- Features to collaborate such as @mentions, and replies with just a single tap.
- Integration of Office 365 products

A *team* site is a collection of people, conversations, files, and tools—all in single place. A subspace in a team site called as *channel*
- Click Teams button on the left side of the app and then pick a team.
- Choose a channel to explore the Conversations, Files, and other tabs.

Figure 2-10. TEAM site

- **Yammer**: It is a platform to facilitate social collaboration in the organization. Yammer is a platform that allows employees to collaborate, connect, and share on their day-to-day work-related matters (Figure 2-11).

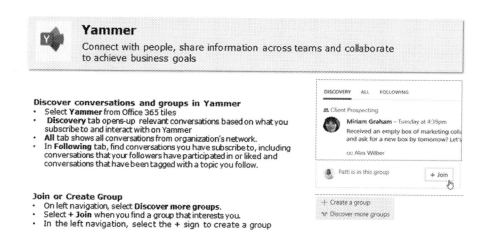

Figure 2-11. *Yammer*

- **SharePoint**: As we have seen in Chapter 1, it is a content management tool that is used to store and retrieve content that employees use to collaborate faster and meet business needs (Figure 2-12).

SharePoint

Share and manage content, knowledge and application to empower teamwork, quickly find information and seamlessly collaborate across organization

Create a Site

- Select whether you'd like to create a Team site or a Communication site.
- Enter the title (and a description, if you want) for the site.
- You can select Edit Image of the pencil icon for editing a flow, and then edit the group email name, if you want.
- Select whether the group will be public or private.
- Choose a sensitivity level for your site information.
- Select a default language for your site and then click Next.
- In the next pane, enter the owners and members.
- Select Finish.

A modern SharePoint Online site is provisioned and ready for use in seconds. If you selected a team site, an Office 365 Group is also created

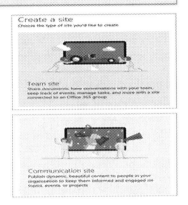

Figure 2-12. *SharePoint*

With this, we conclude our exploration of widely used Office 365 tools. In the upcoming section, we will now explore top SharePoint Online webparts that help us to design sites and thereby create a DCX. Modern organizations have been making investments to create an awesome customer experience (CX) with their products and services. The digital technology revolution has taken CX to another level to form a DCX, which means to provide smooth delivery of products and services and create a wow factor when the customer receives it. In the upcoming chapters, we will take deep dive into DCX to get a clearer picture of it. In this section, we will look into various webparts that help us to create a wow factor for customers.

Embed Yammer Conversations in a SharePoint Online Site

Organization intranets help employees to connect, engage, share ideas, content, and best practices. Integration of Yammer with the help of a Yammer webpart with SharePoint Online sites helps to create communities and foster engagement. Next is an example of a Yammer webpart added to SharePoint Online sites. Yammer helps people to collaborate, connect, and share on business-related stuff in any given moment of time, and with this workplace become collaborative and connected. Through digital collaboration, Yammer helps bring digital transformation, thereby achieving a DCX (Figure 2-13).

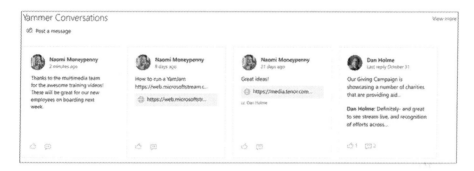

Figure 2-13. *Yammer Webpart*

To add Yammer conversations

1. To embed Yammer feeds of a specific Yammer group into SharePoint Online, copy the Yammer group URL from the browser.

2. Click Edit to make change in the SharePoint Online site.

3. From edit mode, select Yammer webpart to add copied Yammer Group URL.

4. Select Add a group, and in the address box, paste the Yammer group URL (Figure 2-14).

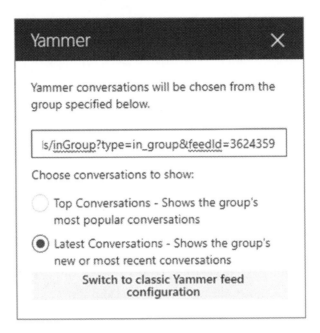

Figure 2-14. *Add Yammer Group URL into Yammer webpart*

Depending upon requirements, select Top Conversations (the group's most engaging conversations), Latest Conversations (group conversations that are new to the reader) and finally save and publish SharePoint Online page.

Once you publish, create a new post by clicking Post a message (Figure 2-15).

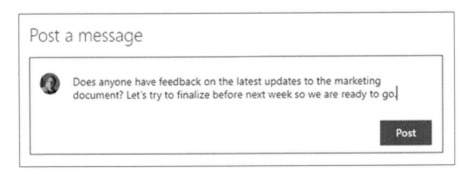

Figure 2-15. *Post message through webpart*

Create a Flow for a List or Library in SharePoint Online

Microsoft Flow is used to set up workflows for lists and libraries in SharePoint Online and OneDrive for Business. To automate common tasks between SharePoint and other Office 365 tools, Microsoft Flow is of great help. With flows, one can create workflows that are simple to use and adopt without any complexities. Gone are the days where developers required a few hundred lines of code to develop a workflow, but with Flow it is just matter of a few seconds and functionality is available at your fingertips. This helps create a DCX.

Steps to create a flow for a list or library:

1. In the SharePoint Online site, navigate to a list or library. The Flow button will exist in the command bar of SharePoint lists and libraries. It is only available for site members who can add and edit on the site, and the option to create a flow will be available.

2. Click Flow then Create a Flow option available at the top of the list or the library (Figure 2-16).

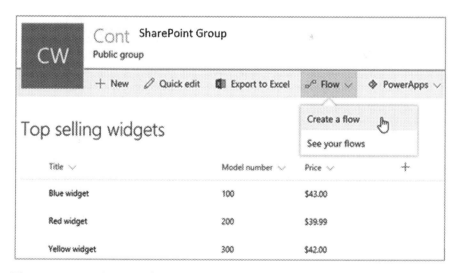

Figure 2-16. *Create Flow*

3. Upon the click of Flow, a flow template will pop up
    on the screen where you will see some commonly
    used flows. Start with common scenarios, such as
    sending a customized email when a new item is
    added to the library. Or, you can choose the custom
    action flow templates.

4. After selecting a template, complete the remaining
    steps on the Microsoft Flow site. Other common
    flows that exist as default send approval emails
    when a new item is added a list, when a post
    appears in a Yammer group or Dynamics, and then
    create a SharePoint list and then save a tweet with a
    specific hashtag to the SharePoint list. Check out the
    flow template in Figure 2-17.

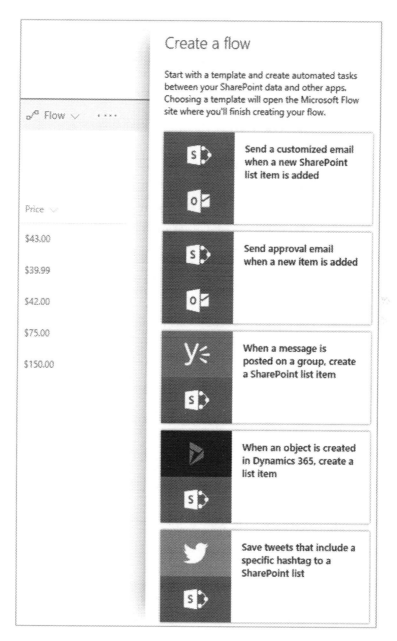

Figure 2-17. Create Flow template

5. Next, follow the instructions on the Microsoft Flow
    site after choosing a specific flow to connect to a
    list or library. For each service used in the flow,
    credentials will be verified. SharePoint and Outlook
    connections will be created automatically.

An example of an action in flow, which is known as a trigger, performs
actions automatically when items are added or changed in a list or library.
The flow template shown in Figure 2-18 sends an email when an item
is added to the list. Depending upon the selection, flows can be started
automatically or manually from the command bar. Default information or
additional information can be added in the flow.

6. In Figure 2-18, select Edit under Send Email to modify
    the default values. The options for the Send Email
    action include changes to how the email looks and
    displaying additional fields from the SharePoint item.

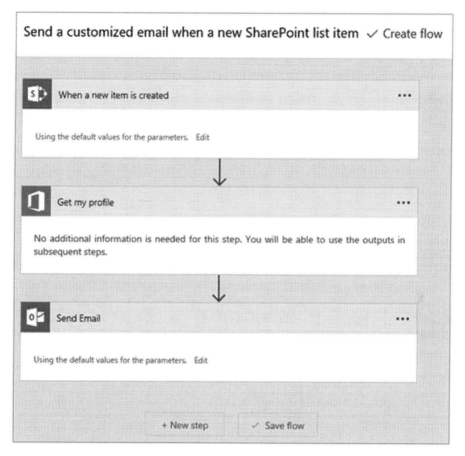

Figure 2-18. *Flow creation*

Adding an email to the list or library will send an email like the one shown in Figure 2-19.

Figure 2-19. *Email triggered through Flow*

Use Microsoft Planner on Your SharePoint Site

As we have seen, Planner is an Office 365 tool that allows you to create boards and team tasks. Planner boards can be used to sort tasks into columns that indicate the progress of tasks over days of the week and sprints. Planner is easy to use as tasks around your board can be moved by just dragging and dropping them. If a task is completed or it needs to be prioritized or shuffled, this can be easily done. Planner boards are useful for communication and to know status updates, as they indicate the current status of each task assigned to you and the rest of your team with respect to completing tasks. Additionally, charts to display your team's progress are available. Planner helps you manage your action plan in a modern way with different features and views thereby providing a DCX. See Figure 2-20.

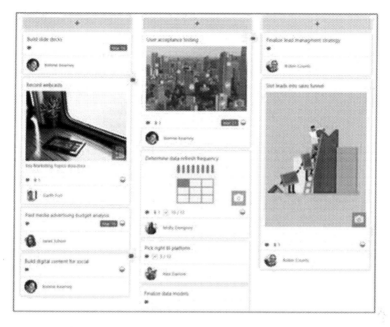

Figure 2-20. *Planner*

Create a plan on your site

1. Go to the SharePoint Online site where you want to add a plan.

2. Click New Plan.

3. Enter a new plan name under Plan name and then click Create.

4. To edit an existing plan, click use an existing plan and then select the plan you want to edit (Figure 2-21).

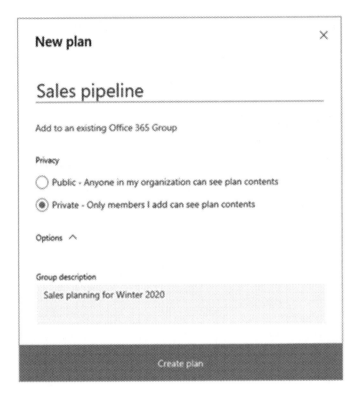

Figure 2-21. *Create Plan*

Use Microsoft Stream in SharePoint Online via a Webpart

Use a Microsoft Stream webpart in SharePoint Online to highlight Stream content in a SharePoint site. Stream is very similar to YouTube; however, it is limited to your organizational boundary, based on the IP address. Stream helps employees to share, reuse, and publish company-related videos in the most efficient ways, which helps to provide a DCX to the internal audience. When we think of a DCX, it is not targeted to external customers but to a combination of organizational employees, direct/indirect customers, suppliers, and organizational fan followers (Figure 2-22).

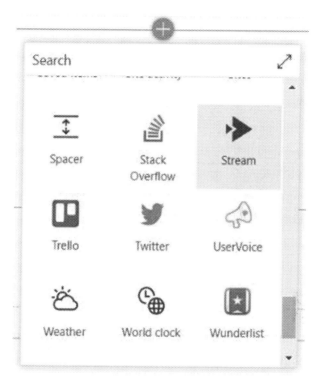

Figure 2-22. *Stream Webpart*

Creating stream video on a SharePoint page

1. Access Stream portal to find the video you want to highlight.

2. Copy the URL / link of the video from the browser's address bar.

3. Then, go to your SharePoint Online site to open the page where you want to add the video.

4. Edit the SharePoint page and add the Stream webpart on your page. Choose source as a single video.

5. Paste in the URL / link to the Stream video in the Video address field (Figure 2-23).

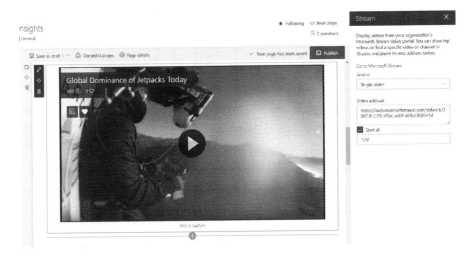

Figure 2-23. *Add Stream in your SharePoint Page*

Use the Bing Maps Webpart

Adding a map to your site has many ways to increase DCX: from the simple "How to find us" to the more complex locations of bikes in a micro-bike hire scheme.

1. Edit the SharePoint Online page to look for the Bing Map webpart.

2. Once choosing a webpart, click Add a title to enter a title for your map.

3. Update the address in the search box.

4. Select either Road, Aerial, or StreetSide view to choose the default view for the map. For Aerial view, you can also choose whether to display labels for all towns, streets, etc.

5. Adjust zoom level for the map, click + or - in the top-left corner of the map (Figure 2-24).

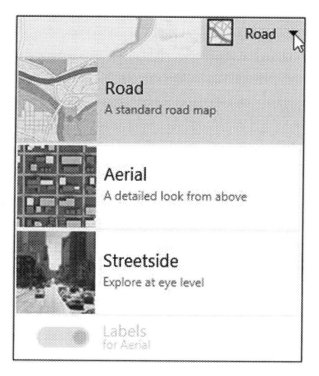

Figure 2-24. *Bing Maps*

Summary

This chapter's exploration of SharePoint features has given us enough understanding to create visually appealing and user-friendly sites to create digital customer experiences. We have just seen a few webparts that can work, but SharePoint Online has plenty of webparts through which the digital customer experience becomes easy. Let's see the overall SharePoint Online webparts list:

Topic:

- Hero – To bring focus and visual interest to your page

- News – Publish eye-catching news, announcements, and updates

- Events to publish upcoming events

- Highlighted content – Distinguish specific content from other content with some filters

Showcase:

- Hero – To bring focus and visual interest to your page

- Image Gallery – To insert an image or collection of images into a page

Blank:

- Bing maps to add maps to maps in pages

- Connectors to receive alerts and messages based on condition you set

- Divider to break line between webparts

- Document library for managing files, that is, to upload, download, and modify on the site

- Embed webpart is used to embed content from other sites

- File viewer to insert files such as Excel, PowerPoint, and PDFs in your pages

- Group calendar to insert Office 365 group calendar

- Kindle instant preview to share preview of Kindle book

- Link to add link to external and internal page

- Microsoft forms to create surveys, quizzes, and polls

- Office 365 video to display video in your communication sites

- People to add select people for contact purposes

- Planner allows you to add teams' actions in your page

- PowerApps to add your customized apps built themselves in PowerApps service

- Power BI to embed report created in Power BI

- Quick Chart to add simple charts in your page

- Quick links to pin items to your page for easy access

- Site Activity to display recent activity on your communication site

- Site to showcase sites on a page, and it will automatically show sites associated to hub site

- Spacer to control vertical space on your page

- Stream to display video from Microsoft stream

- Text to add paragraph, tables, styles, bullets, indentations, highlights, and hyperlinks

- Twitter to display tweets linked to your organization and its interests

- Weather to display current weather on your page

- Yammer to create collaborative experience for your end user

With the exploration journey with Office 365 tools and top SharePoint Online webparts, we are concluding this chapter with plenty of ideas to build awesome SharePoint Online sites for creating high-end value for customers, and therefore create a DCX. In the next chapter, we will study current digital transformation trends, talk about user experience (UX), and customer experience in detail and discuss their benefits.

Apart from standard customer expectations, customers are looking for expectations from rational and emotional sides:

- Price, promotions/offers to get best deals;

- Timing: customer service, delivery to address issues;

- Simple interaction (web, app) for purchase;

- Recommendations to get best product as per needs;

- Loyalty program to retain trust;

- Emotional expectations are honesty, trust, belonging, surprise offers, security, familiarity, reciprocity, and integrity.

Recent Developments in User Experience

User experience was key to many organizations as it gave them a scope for improvement and to be better than competitors. Recent developments in the area of customer experience has been so strong and varied with technology that companies are investing more and more to make them better. There are augmented reality (AR), computer vision, conversational experience, artificial intelligence (AI), natural language processing (NLP), conventional and conversational touch points, Google Home, and Alexa. Organizations are relying upon such technology to create an awesome user experience for their customers. Below are some predictions made by top market research companies.

- Augmented Reality is estimated to be worth $108 billion by 2021. The year 2018 was a breakthrough one for AR. It is becoming a tipping point where it is likely to explode into Main Street and every home will have an AR device or AR-augmented smartphone. Digi- Capital.

- The global machine vision market was valued at $7.91 billion in 2018 and by 2023, the global market is expected to reach $12.29 billion – a compound annual growth rate (CAGR) of 7.61% - `https://www.visiononline.org`

- According to Gartner, more than 50% of organizations will invest in chatbots and bot creations as compared to traditional mobile apps development by 2021.

- Grand View Research has predicted that the chatbot market is expected to reach $1.2 billion on a global scale, in less than ten years. The market will grow at a compounded annual growth rate of more than 24%.

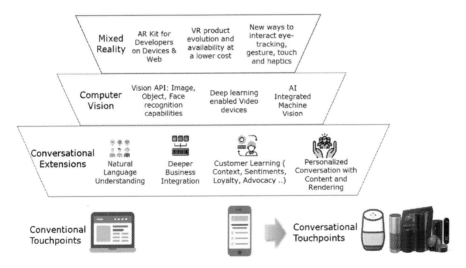

Figure 3-2. *Recent evolution of user experience. The following acronyms are used: VR: Virtual Reality, AR: Augmented Reality, API: Application Programing Interface, AI: Artificial Intelligence. Responsive web application: Application focus on customer understanding*

Figure 3-2 shows different types of the latest digital technology revolution adopted by industries to create maximum impact to enrich the customer experience. Mixed Reality, Computer Vision, and conversational extensions are some of the technologies adopted to enhance the CX. Under a mixed reality AR Kit for Developers on Devices and the Web, for example, an Integrated iOS device camera and motion features produce AR experiences in your app or game, VR product evolution, and availability at a lower cost such as Go Standalone Virtual Reality Headset and New ways to interact eye-tracking, gesture, touch and haptics, which is the science and technology of transmitting and understanding information through touch. Examples are vibration in a mobile phone or the rumble in a game controller, wearables, AR/VR experiences, and automotive infotainment. The second category of computer vision covers Vision API: Image, Object, Face recognition capabilities, for example, Google Cloud Vision API, assign labels to images, and quickly classify them into millions of predefined categories. Deep learning enabled video devices such as AWS DeepLens and AI Integrated Machine Vision, which are used by a camera or multiple cameras to inspect and analyze objects automatically. Conversational Extensions in the case of chatbots cover technology such as Natural Language understanding, sentiments, and personalization.

Understanding customers is about collecting data from customer conversations / journeys and with the help of technology to classify them into insights.

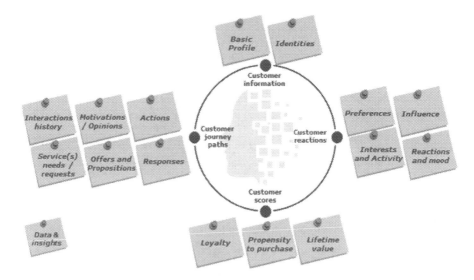

Figure 3-3. Customer Understanding

In Figure 3-3, customer information is captured in terms of a Basic Profile and Identities. Customer journeys are captured in terms of Interactions History, Motivations / Opinions, Actions, Services needs, Offers and Propositions, Responses, and Data and Insights. Customer scores are captured in terms of Loyalty, Propensity to purchase, and Lifetime Value. Customer Reactions are gathered in terms of Preferences, Influence, Interest and Activity, and Reactions and Mood.

Industry Trends with Examples for Digital Customer Experience

In Figure 3-4, we see trends of DCX that are becoming quite popular. Conventional channels such as email continue to exist today. Further, augmented and virtual experiences coming from products such as Alexa or Google are building DCX. Business intelligence reports covering all the facets (demography, social media accounts, choices, and historical transactions) of customers are creating a big impact. A conversational medium using chatbots is creating interaction in the context of real human beings. See Figure 3-4.

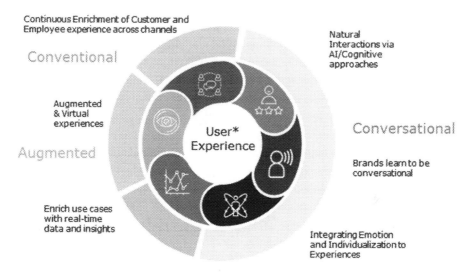

Figure 3-4. *Trends in DCX*

Use Cases for Digital Customer Experience

Figure 3-5 shows various widely used use cases for the DCX such as Making Customer engagement seamless, Employees on the move, Digital Commerce, Employees in Enterprise, Digital Catalogues, and Dealer acceleration.

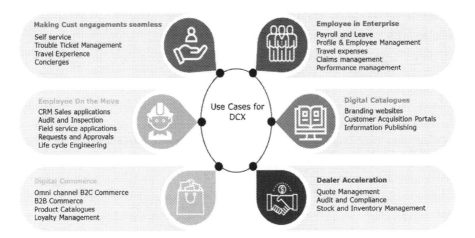

Figure 3-5. *Use case for DCX*

- Making Customer engagement seamless: This covers self-service, Trouble Ticket Management, Travel experience, and Concierges. One of the general areas in this category is self-handling of rescheduling tickets with increasing prices.

- Employee on the move: This covers CRM sales applications, Audit and inspection, Field service applications, Requests and Approvals, and Life-Cycle engineering. In this category, the scope for DCX is employees working on fields as they have minimal access to technology as compared to people who work inside offices.

- Digital Commerce: Omni Channel B2B commerce, Product Catalogues, and Employee Management. The scope of this category includes connecting a business to a business, independent of demographics.

- Employee in Enterprise: Covers Payroll and Leave, Profile and Employee Management, Travel expenses, Claims management, and Performance management. DCX in this area will eliminate dependencies upon Human resources.

- Digital Catalogue: Covers Branding websites, Customer Acquisition Portals, and Information Publishing. SharePoint Online will help in this area.

- Dealer acceleration: Covers Quote Management, Audit and Compliance, and Stock and Inventory Management. In a sector such as Automobiles, it has potential scope for creating a DCX.

How Is the Customer Experience Different from Customer Service?

An employee from a service provider organization is the first point of contact, and he or she is either contacted by a customer by visiting a store or by speaking on the phone; and hence there is a business interaction creating room for the customer experience. This creates an opportunity for the service provider's organization to deliver excellent customer service.

In general, customer service is an aspect of the entire customer experience. For example, if you book a car for a test drive over on the phone and the contact person with whom you are speaking with is friendly and helpful, that's good customer service. In the case of movie tickets, if you arrive early and the cinema offers free popcorn during the show, then that's a good customer experience. That's how the two are different! A customer experience has transformed into a personal touch, friendly interaction, and mutual trust. Thanks to technology, companies can connect with their customers in new and profound ways. Customer

Relationship Management tools help you view a customer's purchase history and to predict future needs even before the customer knows they need it. The ability to predict a future need with tools will let you be proactive and attentive, and it means you can do things like provide similar products based on purchase history, marketing of products, and then get a 360-degree view of the customer.

Customer service still exists as an important factor, but it is no longer the sole focus of a customer experience. Now, a CX brings collaborative ways to strengthen customer relationships using digital technological.

Different Ways to Improve a Digital Customer Experience

As we mentioned earlier, a digital customer experience is all about providing an awesome customer experience using Digital technology such as SharePoint Online. However, Technology being the enabler, it does not mean that it is the only driving force. Primarily, technology remains the primary driving entity to drive DCX, but there are other aspects that we will investigate in detail in this section.

Build a Vision for Customer Experience

The initial step in generating a DCX strategy is to have a customer-focused vision that can translate and communicate to your organization in the most simple terms. The simplest way to build a customer focus vision is to think of creative statements that will serve as guiding principles. For successful organizations, their values are embedded into their culture, style of working, and design of the workplace. Also, it includes wow delivery through execution of service and being open to accept changes. Once principles are laid out, they will drive organizational behavior.

All employees that are part of the organization should be aware and follow these principles by heart, and they should be part of all areas of training and development.

Get an Idea of Who Your Customers Are

The next step in building DCX principles is to inhale and breathe into life the different type of customers your organization is dealing with by developing support teams. If your organization decides to understand customer requirements, then surely they will able to connect and empathize with any circumstances that your customers face. One way to achieve this is by creating personas and giving each persona a name and personality. For example, Lydia is 37 years old, she adores new technology, and she is quite tech savvy enough to follow a video tutorial on her own, whereas Johan (42 years old) can understand and follow clear instructions on a web page. By creating personas, customer support teams can recognize who they are and understand them better. It's also an important step to becoming truly customer centric.

Create an Emotional Connection with Customers

Most people say that when you want to create a DCX, then technology and emotion should connect together. Sometimes, it's not what you say but how you say it in critical crises that matters most. One famous European company was able to connect emotionally with a customer, which turned into a popular story in a business management school. A customer was unable to return a pair of shoes due to her mother's demise. So, the company organized a pick-up for the shoes without a cost and delivered a new pair of shoes as expected within two days. When the company became aware of the mother's demise, they sent a bereavement card to encourage and console the customer.

Research done by the *Journal of Consumer Research* has discovered that more than 50% of the experience is connected to emotion as emotions shape the attitudes that drive decisions. Customers are loyal because they are emotionally attached to a brand or product or service they consume. Businesses that optimize for an emotional connection outperform competitors in sales growth. A study titled "The New Science of Customer Emotions," from *Harvard Business Review* talks about an emotionally engaged customer:

- Likely to recommend your product or service

- Likely to repurchase

- Less likely to shop around

- Much less price sensitive

- Captures customer feedback in real time

One of the ways to capture the DCX is by requesting that the customer answers a customer satisfaction survey, share their story, or capture testimonials. In addition, you can call a customer and request feedback. This activity needs to be performed soon, once the customer request is closed. Sometimes it is good practice to connect customer feedback to a support team member who worked on the requests, and this practice will help to capture performance.

Another is to openly share an escalation matrix with customer so that if they are unhappy, then feedback can be shared openly, and the organization will improve the process.

Quality Management Framework for Team Development

To a DCX for customers, we need to not capture feedback but also implement this feedback; in doing so, a customer will understand that their feedback is valued by the company and will give them a sense of satisfaction. As a company or service provider, it is of prime importance to know what customers think about the quality of the services you offer compared to the customer experience values you have defined for them. Modern organizations or service providers perform feedback assessment based on inputs received over phone and email communications from the customer side. A quality management framework (QMF) will take it one step further by creating a training calendar for a team's development through coaching, eLearning, and group training.

Action Regular Employee Feedback

Many organizations have an annual survey process by which they capture overall feedback from your team on how they handled delivery, customer engagement, and the businesses ability to deliver an exceptional service. In the 11-month survey nothing happens, but continuous employee feedback can play a vital role using feedback tools that will allow teams to openly share improvement ideas on the DCX and for their managers to recommend how teams and leaders are moving toward the business goals. Using platforms such as Yammer or Teams, internal feedback and continuous improvement can be captured and actioned. You can also create a Facebook page or Twitter handle to receive customer feedback on the Web.

Measure ROI from Delivering Excellent DCX

After investing time, money, and energy to build principles for the customer; emotionally connect with the customer; and capturing continuous feedback and processing it, it is of the utmost importance to measure ROI or how it is paying off and what will be revealed in business results. Measuring the DCX experience is one of the biggest challenges faced by organizations. Some companies use the "Net Promoter Score" or NPS, which calculates a score based on a straightforward question asked to a customer based on satisfaction.

Run Projects on Agile Delivery Method

Agile is an industrialized standard adopted by different companies to manage projects. Agile is a philosophy of building products or managing projects based on priority and not developing them end to end. It is a proactive methodology compared to the waterfall model where a reaction takes place after an issue is found. Projects managed using Agile help create a DCX. See Figure 3-6.

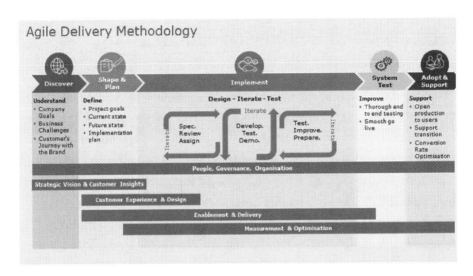

Figure 3-6. *Agile Delivery Methodology*

Agile methodology may vary from company to company but remains aligned toward industry standards. It starts with Strategic Vision and Customer insights, which include understanding company goals, business challenges, and customer journey with the brand. The next phase involves planning and implementation that covers project goals, current state, future state, and implementation plan. A later stage consists of a system test that covers User Acceptance Testing before going live; and finally, a stage consists of measurement and optimization covering the opening production environment to users, support transition, and conversation rate optimization.

DevOps Methodology

Software development projects are now adopting DevOps methodology to build products in an efficient manner. Earlier, there were different and stand-alone phases in the software development cycle such as development, Unit Testing, User Acceptance Test, and deployment; and each one had a dependency for even the smallest development. DevOps has changed entire mindsets and now with this, when some development takes place, it immediately undergoes testing and is deployed into production once the change is approved. Developing products using DevOps creates a strong customer experience as the methodology directs development to what is required by the customer and not by end-to-end development. See Figure 3-7.

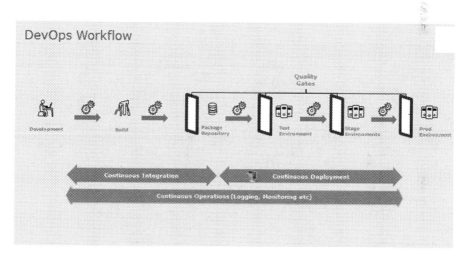

Figure 3-7. *DevOps methodology*

Front-End UX and UI Generate High Levels of Digital Customer Experience

A collaborative design experience enables customer involvement at an experience design stage. This almost totally eliminates the need for reworks at later stages of the program. Rapid prototyping enables design and implements a quick proof of a concept to accelerate a sales or delivery stage. An Application Factory model enables multi-application, multi-use case implementations over the Agile DevOps Framework. Reusable assets, methodologies, and Proof of concept (POC) can be used to accelerate projects. Engaging in innovative programs addresses new experiences like conversations, complex native device features, AR, and leveraging cloud-based microservices models. Figure 3-8 shows focus areas for UI and UX.

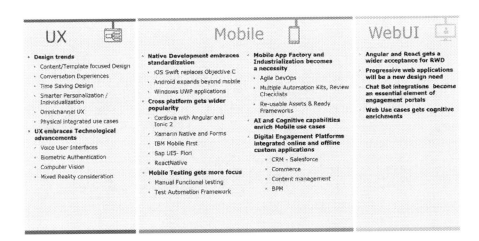

Figure 3-8. *Focus areas of UI and UX*

Applications and Services That Enable DCX Transformation

Figure 3-9 contains a list of applications and services that can generate DCX.

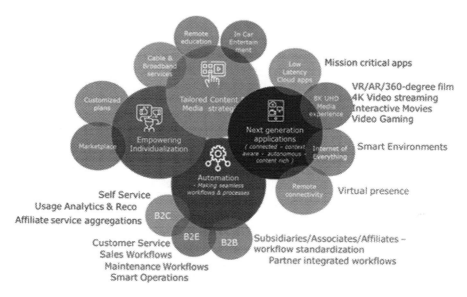

Figure 3-9. *Application and services for DCX*

Upcoming Trends in Digital Customer Experience

Trends falls into categories such as Customer expectations, Enterprise Goals, Customer requirements, and Use cases (Figure 3-10).

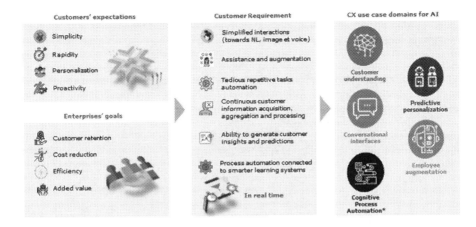

Figure 3-10. *Trends in DCX*

Below are use case descriptions predicted to take place in the near future:

- Conversational interfaces

    - Combination of chat, voice, or any other natural language interface aiming at transforming user interactions into human conversations

- Predictive personalization

    - Methods of delivering to each individual unique experiences and personalized content, both meeting and anticipating his expectations, in real time

- Customer understanding

    - Continuous effort to capture, process, and analyze customers' data in real time from interactions, journeys, events, and emotions in order to build a holistic view of the customer as well as an actionable insight of its needs, expectations, and brand empathy

- Employee augmentation

  - Features augmenting the employee in decision-making and unstructured data analysis, improving his focus on customer-facing activities with more efficiency, reactivity, and relevance

- Cognitive Process Automation

  - Connection of smart learning systems with conventional process automation

Summary

In this chapter, we have touched on various parts of the DCX such as Evolution of DCX, Industry trends, Customer understanding, DCX Use cases, differences between customer service and customer experience, and upcoming Trends in DCX. Now, with experience with SharePoint Online features, Office 365 tools, and DCX, we can start developing smart and intelligent portals using SharePoint Online.

CHAPTER 4

Using UX and UIs to Develop Smart Portals

Until now we have covered SharePoint Online features, Office 365 tools, and looked in-depth toward creating a digital customer experience (DCX). In this chapter, we will focus on building digital portals using SharePoint Online. We will explore both the User Interface (UI) and User Experience (UX) in detail; it's important these are adopted for websites in order to generate DCX. Digital Portals are specialized websites that are smart and intelligent. A fundamental difference between a portal and a website is that a website is hosted on the Internet to drive traffic whereas a portal is developed within an organizational boundary to meet user-specific needs. An example of a website is the company's standard website, and an example of a portal is a sales portal to meet the objective of a sales community. Also in the chapter, we will look at the modern software development life cycle (SDLC), which is getting used to building products such as the SharePoint Online Portal. Using these techniques to build intelligent portals that are eye catching, user oriented, and friendly to navigate are what give us DCX.

© Charles Waghmare 2020
C. Waghmare, *Augmenting Customer Experience with SharePoint Online*,
https://doi.org/10.1007/978-1-4842-5534-6_4

The Software Development Life Cycle

In the area of software development, Figure 4-1 shows the cycle that has been followed for years to develop products. In our experience, we have found this cycle non-flexible as dynamic changes cannot be implemented. As per this cycle, if a product is required to be built, then an analysis needs to be done; followed by defining the requirements; then design and followed by coding, testing, development, and maintenance. In this SDLC, for each step, end-to-end activities need to be completed for the product to be developed before moving into the next step. For example, a requirement analysis of the entire product needs to be completed before it moves to the next step of a requirement definition.

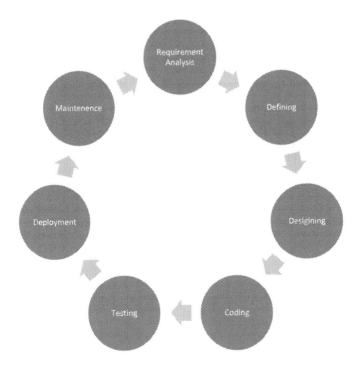

Figure 4-1. SDLC

Scope of dynamic changes are not possible, and, if at all it is required, it must follow the entire SLDC as shown in the figure. With Agile methodology, there is a change in philosophy, and now things are developed when required. Let's say, if we build an X product with Modules A and B then, as per the traditional method, all steps will be followed starting from the requirements, definition, coding, and maintenance for Modules A and B. However, with the Agile approach, Module A or B but not both will be developed as per priority.

Another methodology that is adopted today is DevOps, which is a software development methodology that focuses primarily on integration, communication, and collaboration among IT professionals, which facilitates rapid deployment of products. The DevOps methodology promotes collaboration between the Development and Operations Team and therefore, with such an approach, code deployment to production becomes faster and now there are tools that facilitate deployment in an automated way, thereby increasing an organization's speed to deliver application and services. Let's see the differences between the process shown in Figure 4-1 and Agile.

Traditional Software Development Life Cycle	Agile
Covers end-to-end development of Software products	It is an iterative approach
End-to-end development approach is used to create quality products	It is used as an incremental development approach to build quality products
They have different stages in development	They do have different stages within an incremental development model or methodology

(*continued*)

73

Traditional Software Development Life Cycle	Agile
It suits any size of project	It suits any size but for a small size, results are very evident
It does not allow any immediate or dynamics change in development cycle	It allows changes depending upon priority
It may be complex sometimes if there are too many expectations and tough deadlines	It is very result oriented

Below are the differences between Agile and DevOps:

Agile	DevOps
An iterative approach focused on customer feedback, Team collaboration, and quick releases	Practice that gets development and operations teams together
Management of complex projects	Manage end-to-end development and operations processes
Focus on constant change	Focus on Testing and Delivery
Implemented using tactical frameworks such as SCRUM, Pprint, and safe	There is no common framework as primary goal is collaboration
Training all team members to have same or different skills	Between development and operation teams, DevOps divides and spreads the skills

(continued)

Agile	DevOps
Small Team is a focus of Agile. Smaller team, fewer people with focus on objectives and requests	Involves all the stack holders due to relatively larger team size
Agile development is managed using Sprints and it lasts not more than a month	Deliver code to production every day or every hour
Feedback is submitted by customers	Feedback is given by internal team
Target is Software Development	Fast delivery and business solution
Leverage shift-left	Leverage both shifts left and right
When software is developed and released, Agile team does not care what happens to it	DevOps deals with software that is ready for release and deployed in a reliable and secure manner
Agile doesn't emphasize automation	Automation is the primary goal of DevOps when deploying software
Gap between customer need and development and testing teams are addressed	Gap between development + testing and Ops are addressed
JIRA, Bugzilla, Kanboard are some popular Agile tools	Puppet, Chef, TeamCity OpenStack, AWS are popular DevOps tools
Offers shorter development cycle and improved defect detection	DevOps supports Agile's release cycle

In this section, we will focus on the modern software or application development cycle that is used by to build portals. This cycle is not entirely different as it uses some elements of the traditional approach; however, each approach is different (Figure 4-2).

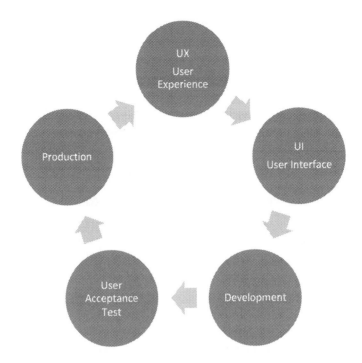

Figure 4-2. *New Development cycle*

User Experience

UX is a design process adopted to build meaningful products to create relevant experiences to users. This process contains the end-to-end design of a product that includes branding, design, usability, and functional aspects of a product.

User Experience is a design process is often interchangeably used with other processes such as UI Design or Usability. User Interface and Usability are significant aspects of UX design, but they are subsets of it as UX design covers plenty of other areas. The typical UX design process covers the end-to-end process of acquiring and combining products that cover significant aspects such as design, branding, function, and usability. Even before a device is in the hands of a user, the user experience is Over.

UX designers not only focus on creating useful products but also on products that give significant pleasure, fun, and efficiency. In addition, there is no specific definition for user experience; therefore, the User experience is an experience that meets user needs in a specific context where they use the product. Let's look at different key factors of the User experience (Figure 4-3).

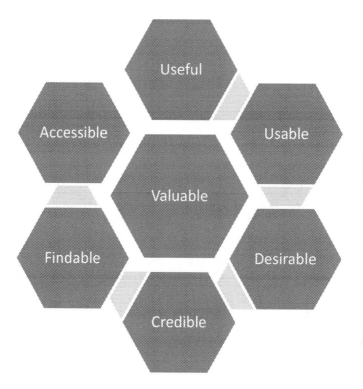

Figure 4-3. *Key factors in User experience*

- Useful: If there is no purpose, then it will unlikely be able to compete for attention. For example, if you buy a car then it should be able to drive you, independent of the day and time.

- Usable: Helps to effectively and efficiently achieve a user's end objective. It makes an impact on safety and is easy to use. A car, for example, should have all features usable before we could drive it.

- Desirable: It is conveyed through, image, branding, colors, font, identity, and emotional design aspect. The more desirable the product, a user creates desire in another user's mind.

- Credible: Ability of a user to trust in the product. Companies producing noncompliant products fall victim to user credibility.

- Findable: Ensure product and its content are easy to find. Netflix helps a user to find the best online show based on an internal algorithm.

- Accessible: Provides a user experience that can be accessed by users of a full range of abilities. Company manufacturing product with listening, hearing, and speaking abilities, for example, does have greater accessibility. Accessibility means designing a product for every type of user.

- Valuable: Must deliver value to the business and to the customer.

Why, What, and How

Now we look at why, what, and how as part of a UX design (Figure 4-4).

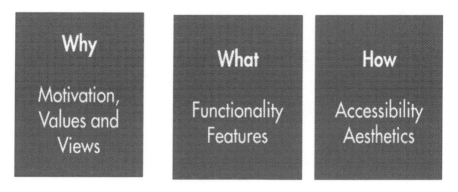

Why, What, How of UX Design

Figure 4-4. *Why, What and How for UX*

Generally, a UX designer considers the why, what, and how of a product's use.

- The "Why" factor involves user motivation, values, and views for product adoption, which could relate to a task that a user performs associated with ownership and use of the product.

- The "What" factor focuses on product functionality.

- Finally, the "How" factor deals with the accessibility and aesthetics of products.

UX designers start with the Why factor before defining the What and then, finally How factor, to build products with an awesome user experience. In software product design, one must make sure that a product's substance comes through an existing device and should offer a seamless, fluid experience.

UX Design Is User Centered

UX design covers the entire user experience journey as it is multidisciplinary. Typically, the background of a UX designer comes from fields such as visual design, programming, psychology, and interaction design. When you are designing for humans, potential human challenges such as reading small text, colors, sizes, and others are taken into consideration. The job of UX designers is to perform user research, create personas, designing wireframes and interactive prototypes as well as testing designs. Such tasks are likely to vary from one company to other, but they want designers to be user focused, advocate for users, and always keep the user as the focal point for all design and developmental efforts. Consequently, most users work in such a way that all relevant needs of users are addressed. To perform a UX assessment and conclusion, user-centric design steps shown in Figure 4-5 can be followed.

UX User centric design

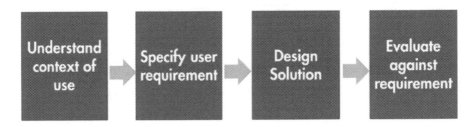

Figure 4-5. *Steps to be followed for UX*

User Interface

Now we are at the second stage of the modern development cycle called User Interface (UI). UI is a place where a user interacts with the design. Control panels, dialog boxes, faces, and voice-connected faces are some examples of Graphical User Interfaces (GUIs). Engaging users with 3D design using body motions are an example of a gesture-based interface. UI is an essential part of UX. Typically, a user gives feedback on design, likeability, and usability. With a higher user focus, designers can build highly usable and efficient designs. Understanding different user scenarios will make designers aware of future flaws and make design very robust. Ideally, UI design should not be device specific, but they should focus on how a user interacts with a design. UI should be designed in such a way that all possible features can be observed quickly, and it should be readily used by users.

If a user experiences a product's features, then UI is diligently developed. Frequently confused with UX design, UI design deals with the surface design of a product and overall feel of a design. Also, UX has a scope that covers the total spectrum of the UI (Figure 4-6). One analogy is to imagine UX design as a car with UI design as the leg room. Normally, in GUIs, to convey your organization's values and maximize usability, you should create pleasing aesthetics and animations.

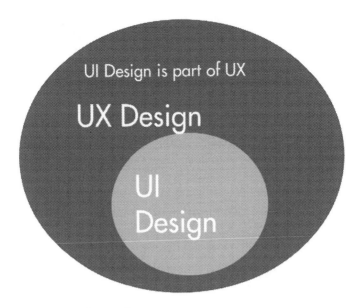

Figure 4-6. *UI is subset of UX*

To create awesome impressive GUIs, think – users are human, therefore they need comfort and low cognitive loads. Follow the below guidelines:

- Use elements such as buttons to perform predictably so users can unconsciously use them everywhere. Form should follow function.

- Preserve high discoverability. Clearly label icons.

- Maintain interfaces clearly and simply. Create an invisible feel. Every element should have a purpose.

- Respect a user's eye and attention. Focus on the hierarchy and clear readability.

- Minimize the number of alignment lines. Choose Justified text.

- Draw attention using color, brightness, and contrast. Avoid excessive use of colors or buttons.

- Further, draw attention by using text via font sizes such as bold type/weighting, italics, capitals, and distance between letters.

- Users should read content meanings by scanning.

- Minimize user actions to perform tasks.

- Provide guidance to users by indicating preferred actions.

- Make use of chatbot in the UI in order to create smooth user engagement.

- Add defaults to reduce user burdens (e.g., pre-fill forms).

- Manage user behavior related to navigation and search function using reusable design patterns.

- Maintain brand consistency.

Following these UX and UI steps, development teams can use out-of-the-box SharePoint Online features such as features webparts and the Office 365 tool that we explored in the first two chapters of this book. Further, they can customize components using code. With such UI development standards, development will hand over portals to a User Acceptance Team (UAT), who will perform tests under valid test cases and post implementation of UAT feedback, the system will go live.

To understand UI, let's do an assessment of the portal by performing UI assessment. In the below examples, we have created a dummy SharePoint portal, over which we will perform UI assessment. In the below images, the numbered text represents the assessment and is followed by its answer.

Scenario 1

This scenario deals with font size and color scheme chosen, which are affecting the overall design (Figure 4-7).

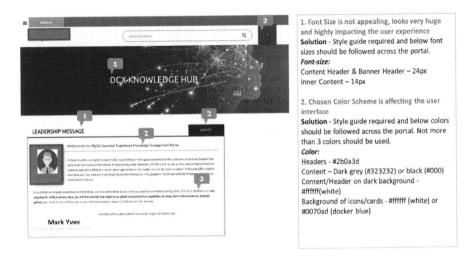

Figure 4-7. Scenario dealing with font size and color size

Scenario 2

This scenario deals with unnecessary navigation, white spaces, and margins, as shown in Figure 4-8.

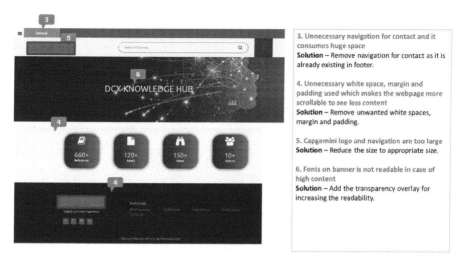

Figure 4-8. *Scenario dealing with size of objects*

Scenario 3

It deals with space (Figure 4-9).

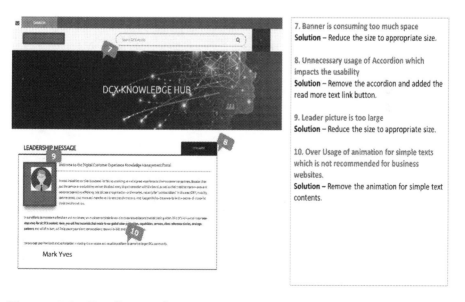

Figure 4-9. *Dealing with space*

Scenario 4

It deals with buttons and features (Figures 4-10 and 4-11).

11. Footer is too large with white spaces and padding instead of content, which is not recommended.

12. Cards in explore section is very big and not much impressive
Solution – Reduce the size and provide proper alignment.

13. Content area of Cards in explore section is not clickable
Solution – Should make it clickable

14. Key figures color scheme is not appealing, and the purple color is not getting suited for the flow of the webpage
Solution – Should Follow color scheme as in point number 2

Figure 4-10. *Deals with buttons and feature*

15. Usage of two <a> in cards section for same purpose is not recommended
Solution- Wrap all the elements using a <div> and wrap that <div> using <a>.That is the good coding standard.

16. Even though the web pages are developed using Bootstrap 4, it is not fully responsive due to insufficient coding standard.
Solution- Additional work needed to optimize the code by following W3C standards to overcome this issue and it may result into developing the portal from the scratch with all required supporting environments.

Figure 4-11. *Scenario dealing with buttons and features*

Note   In the comments in Figure 4-11: Bootstrap means development done using open source Cascaded Style Sheet (CSS) framework, and insufficient coding standard refers to the static coding method and not the dynamic method.

Scenario 5

It deals with features (Figure 4-12).

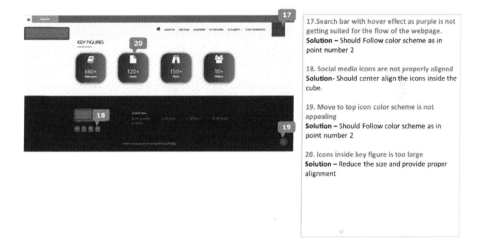

Figure 4-12. Deals with features

Summary

In the modern development cycle, we have UX and UI components of development with a substantial amount of focus. Subsequent components such as Development, UAT, and Deployment have standard understanding. Development will be performed by a technical team, and the User community and business will perform UAT and provide sign-off; and then finally, changes are deployed in production. In this chapter, we have looked at the UI and UX aspects in detail and this will be useful from a product standpoint.

CHAPTER 5

Building Knowledge systems Using SharePoint Online

In the previous chapter, we focused on User Interface (UI) and User Experience (UX), in order to developed a smart portal or website to create a digital customer experience. Until now, with experience in SharePoint Online features and, specifically, webparts; Office 365 tools, and building customer experience, we will discover a smart Knowledge Management system build in SharePoint Online called Solution Database, which helps store, reuse, and create knowledge, in particular, for an incident management process. We will also explore another Knowledge Management system: Ask the Expert tool, built in SharePoint Online for consultants to gain expert opinions from experts. And finally, we will look at Communities of Practices in order to create a knowledge-sharing culture using SharePoint Online. We will also see the benefit of introducing Communities of Practice initiatives, which are an important element in Knowledge Management (KM) practice, and check out its implementation using SharePoint Online.

© Charles Waghmare 2020
C. Waghmare, *Augmenting Customer Experience with SharePoint Online*,
https://doi.org/10.1007/978-1-4842-5534-6_5

Incident Management Process

This process is defined as finding a workaround or quick fix whenever there are faults or issue in the system. Imagine that you are running daily jobs to populate your database and produce reports. It may happen that reports are not getting published as the database did not update; or due to an erroneous file, daily jobs are failing. These situations are called incidents, and the incident management process helps to find quick fixes or workarounds to fix these incidents in a minimum amount of time.

Incidents are classified as per priorities. Normally, a Priority 1 (P1) incident has 8 hours for resolution time, Priority 2 (P2) has 16 hours for resolution time, Priority 3 (P3) has 24 hours for resolution time, and Priority 4 (P4) has 48 hours for resolution time. As shown in Figure 5-1, there is an impact urgency matrix and based on that, the priority is calculated. There are serious service-level agreements between vendors and service providers for penalties whenever there is a violation of the time required to take care of incidents.

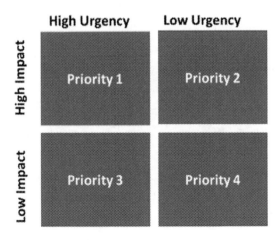

Figure 5-1. *Impact Urgency Matrix*

Solution Database – An Introduction

As seen in Figure 5-2, there are teams: Team 1 to Team 5, and they have used the same solution; however, each of them has taken a different amount of time to implement a solution. For example, Team 3 has used the maximum time to implement a solution whereas Team 2 has taken the minimum 1 hour to implement a solution. There are various reasons for variations in time differences for Team 2 and Team 3. In the case of Team 3, a solution did not exist, and the team was required to create such a solution and test it before deployment. In the case of Team 2, there was a system where reusable solutions were getting maintained, and therefore Team 2 was able to reuse a solution that had already been implemented; so that is why their resolution time was the quickest.

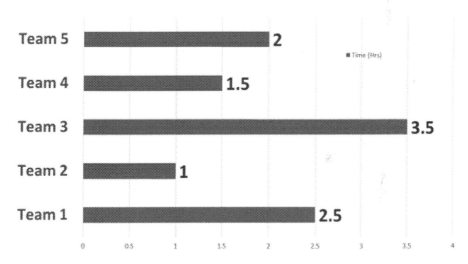

Figure 5-2. *Time range of solution between teams*

The secret of Team 2 in the implementation of a solution follows KM Practice. They were maintaining a database called a solution database where new solutions were getting stored, and existing solutions were getting reused when needed. Therefore, their resolution time went down.

In the upcoming section, we will design a Solution Database (SDB) and replicate this design in SharePoint Online for smooth functioning. To design, we assume that we are creating solution data for an incident management process so that there is a faster resolution time for incident closures, which will increase customer satisfaction.

Solution Database Definition

Solution Database is a KM tool that ensures knowledge created through transactions such as incidents, which are captured, are categorized and stored in the solution database for future reuse. The solution database allows the user to search for existing solutions of past incidents that can be reused for future incidents. It includes solutions for tickets from all ticketing tools that are subsequently validated by Subject Matter Experts (SMEs). The following is the purpose of the Solution Database to improve productivity through reduction in the time for solving incidents:

- Build knowledge bases of reusable solutions for long-term advantage

- Authentic solutions ensure quality resolutions of any future incidents

- Quick and effective retrieval of required solutions at the time of need

- Increase service quality

- Frequently reused solutions lead to standard solutions and generic problems

- Drive sharing and reuse as cultural change

Knowledge Needs to Have a Solution Database

As we seen so far, a solution database is a repository of transaction knowledge built up from incidents. In addition, SDB has different reasons for being developed. Let's check out some of them:

- Capture past resolutions: incidents, problems, enhancements

- Project documentation across value chain

- Just stay abreast and stay connected with peers

- Locate expertise and seek answers

- Learning (process / tools/ technology

- Quality and Standards of Performance Working Protocol

- Understand Business Processes/deliverables

- Know your customers /Feedback

- Monitor performance (BU, process, individuals)

- Hybrid of Process, Product- and Service-centric KM models

- Identify an organization's core process

- Build knowledge bases for long-term advantage

- Connect islands of knowledge: creators, seekers, enablers, SMEs

- Knowledge inputs at time of need

- Focus on Transactional, Tacit, and External Knowledge

- Peer-to-peer connection beyond geographies

- Drive sharing and reusage as cultural change

- Measure business benefits

SDB Architecture

So far, we have seen the definition, objectives, and different knowledge needs of a solution database. For convenience, we will assume an existing solution database for incident management purposes, which will help us to understand more clearly, and readers are welcome to generalize for other purposes for their different knowledge needs. In this section, we intend to define solution database architecture more clearly to understand how we can create a new solution and reuse existing ones from SDB. Figure 5-3 is an overview of SDB architecture.

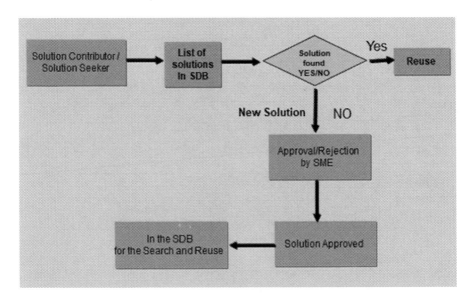

Figure 5-3. *Solution Database Architecture*

In Figure 5-3, we see a Solution Contributor or Solution Seeker access SDB to resolve incidents. In the case where a solution seeker discovers a list of solutions with the help of search, he or she is able to pick and choose a relevant solution from the list of solutions in the database. In the case where a solution does not exist, the seeker is encouraged to a create a new solution that gets reviewed from a SME before it is available for all users. Architecture of SDB is based on two principles of KM, that is, reuse knowledge and create knowledge.

Designing such architecture on SharePoint, then with Workflows, and now with Flows has become an act of simplicity with a default set of features available in SharePoint technology that facilitates the design SDB architecture.

Building an SDB

Now we have come to the crux of this chapter where we will learn to create and reuse solutions in a solution database for the incident management process. Again, for convenience, we will assume an SDB is for the incident management process, and solutions will be created to fix incidents in a timely manner. Let's begin with creating a solution using SharePoint Online Forms that can be linked with Flows to trigger events and notifications.

It is very important that we a create structure that is easy to understand and convenient for adding solution details. Therefore, as mentioned in the above paragraph, we use forms to capture a solution and metadata about the solution. Figure 5-4 is an example of a form that can be used to capture solutions for the incident management process and is suitable for an IT service organization that specializes in application maintenance support for business. Let's look at the form to capture incidents and fields used in the form. Solutions are stored in an actual SharePoint Online object called a list and are retrieved based on a standard or advanced search.

* Fields are Mandatory

	OK Cancel

📎 Attach File	🍄 Spelling...	
Solution Type	New Solution ▾
ReferenceTicketID*	
TicketType*	▾
Customer*	▾
LegacySystem	▾
Software Platform / Tools	▾
Symptom*	

Analysis	▾
Solution (Keywords)*	
Programming Language	▾
Operating System	▾
Database System	▾
Factory*	▾
Service Area*	▾
GPC*	▾

	OK Cancel

Figure 5-4. *Form to create solution in Solution Database*

With reference to Figure 5-4, let's try to understand what each field means (you can customize this form to your requirments). The above form was created from the author's real-time experience working with SDB implementation for a large German organization to streamline an incident management process for an application maintenance services SAP business.

- **Solution Type -**

    - **New Solution**: If it's your own solution used to resolve the incident then, select the solution type as New Solution.

- **Reuse**: If existing solution / standard solution from the solution database is used to resolve the incident then, select the solution type as Reuse.

- **Workaround (Standard Solution)**: If the temporary solution is given to circumvent or prevent a known error from occurring, then select the solution type as Workaround (Standard Solution).

- **ReferenceTicketID**: The Ticket ID of the incident from the ticketing tool.

- **TicketType**: The Ticket type of the incident from the ticketing tool.

- **Customer**: The name of customer/Project.

- **LegacySystem**: A legacy system is an existing application system with poor compatibility with modern equivalents. For example, any system that is being rammed down / sunsetting, or being phased out, but still in use depending on the business requirement.

- **Application**: Application software is computer software designed to help the user perform a particular task. It differs from an operating system and a programming language.

- **Software Platform**: A software platform describes the basic software system or software framework (including application frameworks), which allows software to run or from which the software application is built up.

- **Symptom**: It is the error code reported in the ticket in the ticketing tools.

- **Analysis**: Investigating the error reasons using the business-related know-how.

- **Solution (Keywords)**: These are the apt words that will help the search engine to find the solution. The Criteria are –

  - Transaction Code -

  - Transaction Name -

  - Business Scenario -

  - Error Code -

  - Program Name / Interface -

  - Special function - like „CIP2SAP"

  - Version of SAP Syst"

- **Programming Language**: Examples are C++, Java, SQL, ABAP, ..."

- **Operating System**: Indicate what operating system (OS) the problem occured on.

- **Database System**: Enter name of database.

- **Factory**: Enter name of factory or resource group details.

- **Service Area**: Name of the service area.

- **GPC**: Global Production Center – Normally, these are gloabal delivery centers working in the form of a resource pool.

The search engine looks only for appropriate keywords in the field of Solution (Keywords) as seen in Figure 5-5. Fill in this field very accurately. Solution (Keywords) must contain all keywords listed in Figure 5-5 known by the user.

1.Transaction Code	List all affected transaction codes
2. Transaction Name	Short description of the transaction
3. Business Scenario	Name of business scenario used inside transaction
4. Error Code	Name of error code
5. Program Name / Interface	Name of program / interface (techn. name)
6. Special Function	like „CIP2SAP"
7. Version of SAP System	like „4.7C", „ECC6.0"
8. Module Name	Name of the Module (e.g. „TT")
9. Important Keyword	like „Change Contract' or „Related Records"
10. Version of Non-SAP System	

Figure 5-5. *Specific descriptions of the keywords the user can type in Solution (Keywords)*

Figure 5-6 is an example of a solution created containing information updated in all fields. OSD stands for operation service desk, which is a ticketing tool where incidents or faults are maintained.

KB ID	KB00000022959
Solution Type	New Solution
ReferenceTicketID	HD0000008046610
Reference KB ID	
TicketType	Fault
Symptom	Perfecseal Mankato is concerned with the manner that packaging materials are being back flushed in SAP. The BOMs have been setup with the Net ID flag checked. This is calculating the expected number of packaging materials to be consumed and purchased based on the delivered quantity. The problem is occurring when parts are produced. BMS or SAP is calculating a back flush quantity based on the total quantity (which includes scrap) instead of the delivered quantity. This is causing a partial unit of a material to be back flushed instead of the expected full unit. Therefore, inventory is being overstated since we are actually consuming a full unit. In one month on one material, user were 1,000 units less than what SAP indicated. What do user need to do in order to have SAP backflush the way the materials are being planned?
Analysis	In order 134009, since the net id indicator in the material master of components to be back flushed is set, the system is calculating the component requirement quantity on the basis of total quantity - scrap portion. In order to have a component back flush same as that planned for the component, we should remove the net id indicator.
Solution	In order 134009, since the net id indicator in the material master of components to be back flushed is set, the system is calculating the component requirement quantity on the basis of total quantity - scrap portion (42,429 - 3,819 = 38,610). With the net indicator set for the component for example: 300000005936, the planned component quantity is 78 pc but the actual back flushed quantity if 71.578 pc (when confirmation of 38,610 is done). In order
Solution (Keywords From OSD)	Component backflush with Net ID indicator.
Related Tickets	
Consultant	gautam.varma@siemens.com
Customer	Bemis, US
LegacySystem	
Software Platform / Tools	
WorkGroup	
Programming Language	
Operating System	
Database System	
Factory	LOG
Service Area	PRODUCTION_PROCESS
GPC	GPCI

Figure 5-6. *An approved solution in SDB*

Searching an SDB

Now we know how to create solutions in a SharePoint-based solution database system. Let's try to discover how we can search for solution in an SDB. The solution database allows the user to search for existing reusable solutions of incidents and problems. Figure 5-7 is example of s standard search.

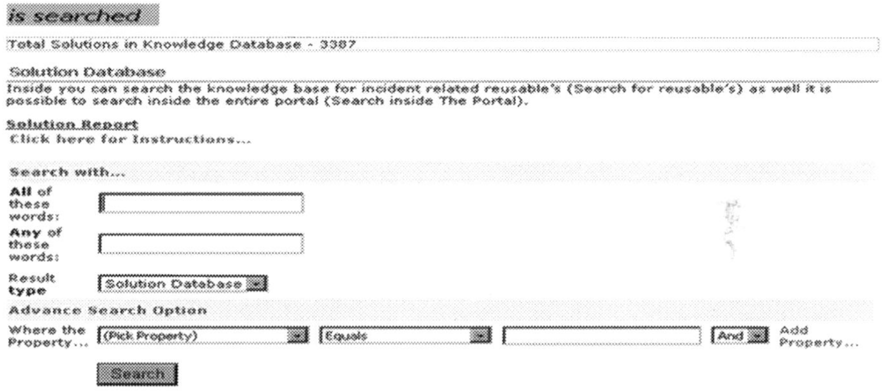

is searched

Total Solutions in Knowledge Database ~ 3387

Solution Database
Inside you can search the knowledge base for incident related reusable's (Search for reusable's) as well it is possible to search inside the entire portal (Search inside The Portal).

Solution Report
Click here for Instructions...

Search with...

All of these words:	
Any of these words:	
Result type	Solution Database

Advance Search Option

Where the Property... (Pick Property) | Equals | | And | Add Property...

Search

Figure 5-7. *Searching solution in SDB*

The user can search for information by typing their keyword (e.g., SAPPORO) in the boxes present in Figure 5-7. The user will then view the list of solutions in the SDB with the provided keyword (Figure 5-8). The user can search for solution(s) by typing a reference ticket number from a ticketing tool or a description of the problem as the keyword.

Figure 5-8. *Search Result*

Figure 5-9 is an example of an advanced search in an SDB where the user can search using parameters such as customer or factory or GPC.

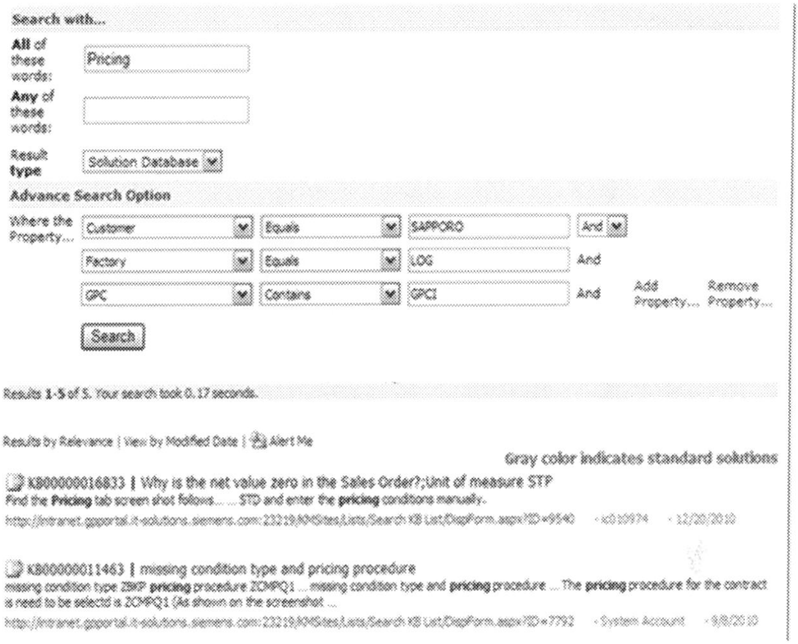

Figure 5-9. *Advanced Search Result*

If no solution is found (Figure 5-10), then solve the problem yourself and then contribute the solution in the SDB.

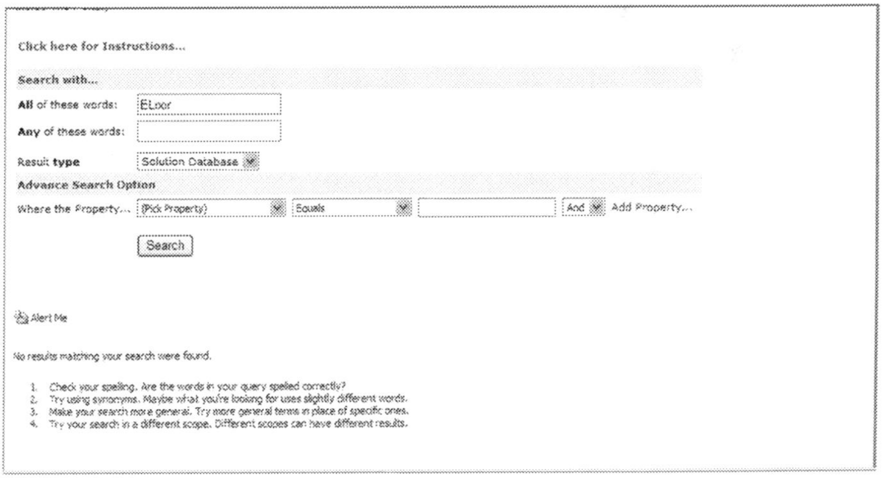

Figure 5-10. *If no solution is found*

Reusing the Solution

Until now we have seen how to create a solution and search for a solution in an SDB. Let's see how we can reuse an existing solution from the SDB. If a relevant solution is found, then reuse it (Figure 5-11).

KB ID	KB00000016597
Solution Type	
ReferenceTicketID	RI0001772865
TicketType	Incident
Symptom	The user needs to receive orders of authorized purchases, in PDF format because she replaces her partner.
Analysis	Check the messages of purchase order with transaction ME23N, complete number of purchase order and press enter. Then press message bottom, check Output Type "ZAEM" (Arg Purch.order mail), funtion partner and partner fields. Check Vendor data master with transaction XK03 (the vendor is the same to partner number) and complete company code, press enter.
Solution	The first step shoud be created the vendor data master of new partner so that go receiv the mail. Modify with transaction MN05 , I complete Output type field, with the value "ZAEM", press enter, then select key combination "Purchasing Group Print", press enter. Complete Purchase organization field and execute or F8. Finally modify partner number and save.
GPC	GPCM
Service Area	INVENTORY_PROCUREMENT
Number Of Reuses	0
Software Platform / Tools	SAP
Problem Title	

Content Type: Item
Created at 12/4/2010 2:15 by System Account
Last modified at 12/4/2010 2:15 by System Account

[Reuse]   [Close]

Figure 5-11. *Solution Database*

In order to create a reusable solution, there is an important element called myRatings that captures user points based on a new solution created or reused that provides some encouragement for users to remain engaged in the SDB.

- For each new solution, 10 points get added to the user's myRatings.

- After the review and approval, the user earns 5 points per proposed solution.

- For Reuse - 10 points.

- For Workaround Solution – 15 points.

Figure 5-12 shows this.

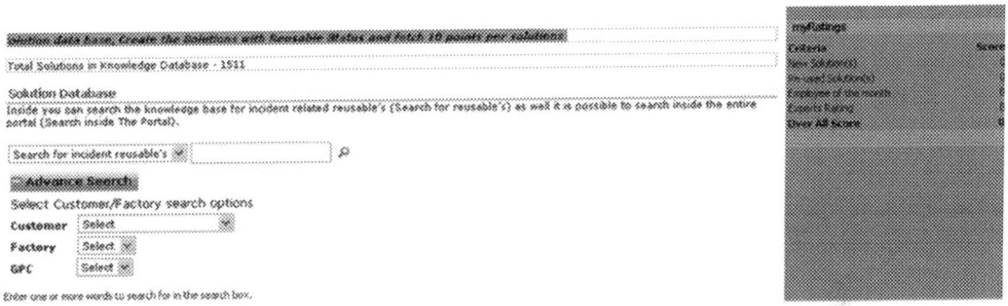

Figure 5-12. *User myRatings*

Ask the Expert

A solution database may not be the ideal to discover all solutions in an SDB. Therefore, Ask the Expert can help users to get to closer to a solution. Ask the Expert enables any user to ask and post any question or any official query in regard to the content of functional and technical issues. If the user has a query regarding a specific problem and can't find an answer within a solution database, the user should use "Ask the Expert."

If the query is new, then the user should select the New status (Figure 5-13). If it is an existing query that needs a more detailed response, the user should select Reopen as the status.

Figure 5-13. *Ask the Expert Form*

Below are the descriptions of the fields that need to be filled out to post a query.

Title	**Enter the subject of the problem you are facing.**
Factory	**Select from the drop-down the name of the Factory.**
Query	**Post your detailed query here.**
Response from Expert	**The expert will provide his or her response here.**
Query status	**The status of the query when being modified needs to be selected from the drop-down.**
Priority	**The priority of the issue can be selected from the drop-down.**

Experts view in the admin portal (only viewable by an expert) where all the questions/queries posted by portal users that are active and will be visible in this module for the expert users (Figure 5-14). A delete option will be provided as well. Expert users can edit any of the queries and provide answers for the same. The field names and their description will be the same for all the experts.

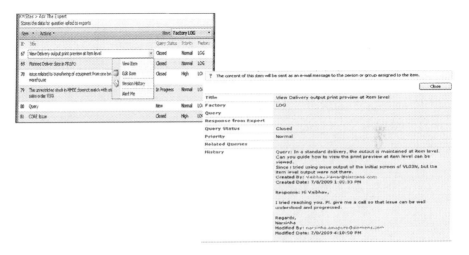

Figure 5-14. *An example of Ask the Expert*

When a new query is raised, an email notification is sent automatically to the expert list of the respective factory. If there is any change in the status of the query, an email notification is sent to the experts and the requestor. If the problem is solved by the expert, the requester receives a notification that their query is answered and that they can look up the solution. Therefore, the requester has to go again to Ask the Expert and open the item. If the response is acceptable, the query is solved, and the status should be changed to Closed. If not, the requester should specify the problem and send the query again. The experts will receive another notification that they have to work on this again.

Besides that, it is always possible to reopen a closed query. In the field History, the query-response interaction will be generated automatically, including details about who edited the query and when. This responded to query should now be uploaded by the requester to the solution database.

Advantages of an SDB

Let's look at some advantages of an SDB:

- Avoid reinvention. Quick replication between different global teams.

- Drive reusage of knowledge.

- Standardize processes for common delivery pool.

- Improves **contextual grasp** of customer knowledge.

- Move up from customer satisfaction to **customer delight.**

- Learn right things with the right speed and ensure financial benefits (P2P learning).

- Faster collaboration among teams and high levels of employee engagements.

- Improve operational efficiency (Productivity, Response time, Optimize utilization of resources).

- Smart work ways to ensure market growth from existing customers.

Application Management/Maintenance competition is getting fiercer and players are now increasingly emphasizing more on building and sustaining competitive advantages. Organizations have been quick to realize the fact and started focusing on systems and processes that help consultants in keeping their knowledge abreast and thereby becoming more productive and effective for their customers. Reusable systems aim to ensure consistent, efficient, effective, and smart services to end customers by enabling smart work ways within organizational delivery units. It also improves the productivity of consultants in the following ways:

- Ensures error-free / first time right (FTR) work ways

- Ensures new joiners adapt faster and minimizes less impact on delivery to customer

- Common delivery pool offers source of knowledge and documentation, which results in higher flexibility

- Enhance chances for cross-selling and upselling by sharing across all customer accounts

- Improved SLAs and response time due to reduced information search time

- Drive standardization across processes

Introduction to Communities of Practice

A **Community of Practice (CoP)** is a group of people who share a craft and/or a profession. The group can evolve naturally because of the members' common interest in a particular domain or area, or it can be created specifically with the goal of gaining knowledge related to their field. It is through the process of sharing information and experiences with the group that the members learn from each other, and have an opportunity to develop themselves personally and professionally – **Wikipedia.**

CoP is an initiative that helps create and cultivate knowledge, thereby creating a knowledge-sharing culture in the organization.

What do CoPs do?

- Facilitate collaboration among members
- Answer questions via SMEs
- Capture knowledge and reuse it
- Prevent reinventing the wheel by sharing knowledge
- Share successful best practices
- Filter out incorrect information

Key CoP features:

- Shared domain of practice or interest
- Crosses operational, functional, and organizational boundaries
- Defined by knowledge and not tasks
- Managed by collaboration and making connections
- Focus on value, exchange, and learning

The successful creation of a CoP would need proper planning and ideally needs to follow the phases below:

1. Identify the audience, purpose, goals, and vision for the community.

2. Define the activities, technologies, and processes that will support the community's goals.

3. Plan specific activities for the target audience for the initial stages of the CoP building.

4. Roll out the community to a broader audience over a period of time.

5. Engage members in collaborative learning, knowledge sharing activities, and networking events.

Active CoP participation helps increase the organizational knowledge base, which helps improve our capabilities and provide better business value, mentioned below in the area of team, people, and processes:

- Reduce rework and avoid reinventing the wheel by capturing and sharing best practices;

- Connects team members across locations and helps promote teamwork and collaboration;

- Helps increase idea creation and solve issues in projects;

- Easy centralized access to important information, documents, and SME lists;

- Effective forum for collaborating and staying up to date in area of expertise;

- Knowledge sharing happens across organizational and geographic boundaries;

- KM tools available for networking and strengthening relationships;

- For junior members, CoPs provide an ideal forum to expand their skills and expertise and reduce their learning curve on new concepts;

- Collaboration tools help bring ideas into the organization faster and improve the rate of innovation;

- Helps create a culture of openness and also recognizes top contributors.

Value of CoPs for Delivery Teams

A successful CoP initiative revolves around business value, community participation, increased knowledge, and improved capabilities as seen in Figure 5-15. Beyond this platform, content, people, and process are other important aspects for a CoP's success.

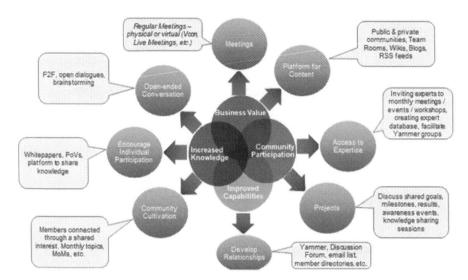

Figure 5-15. *A successful Communities of Practice*

Community Development Life Cycle

A community development life cycle is divided into inception, establishment, growth, and maturity as explained below.

Inception

- Create KM portal detailing the purpose, goals, and vision for the community;

- Spark initial engagement from the CoP members to be part of the community and contribute;

- Promote community through various channels to increase participation.

Establishment

- Regular communications and surveys to CoP members to create awareness on planned initiatives and gather feedback on CoP,

- Initiatives can be tailored according to the feedback and specific needs of the CoP members,

- Webcast series on hot topics can be presented by CoP SMEs.

Growth

- Higher levels of interaction and engagement from the CoP members and growing sense of belonging to the community,

- Social media tools like Yammer for more interactions between CoP members,

- Quarterly Newsletters with latest news related to CoP to be sent to community members.

Maturity

- Community becomes more self-sustaining over a period of time,

- Volunteer-led activities like organizing regional Face-to-Face meetings on specific CoP topics,

- Recognition programs can be launched for CoP members depending on the budget.

Community Roles and Responsibilities

For a successful CoP initiative, there are designated roles that help community facilitation and attends its objectives. Below are the roles described in detail.

- **CoP Sponsor** is able to envision the purpose and vision of the community and also foresee the goals of the CoP over time, and should have a sense of how the CoP can interact across Capgemini.

- **CoP Facilitator** helps with building, connecting, guiding and facilitating the overall community.

- **CoP Leader** helps communicate the CoP goals and vision and provides continuous support for the community.

- **CoP Core Group** is a working group that helps with the CoP start-up activities and continues to provide ongoing support.

- **CoP Experts** are the SMEs within the CoP.

- **CoP Members** are the essence of the community as without them the CoP would not exist.

Communities Are Powerful Tools, As Long As You Put Members' Needs First – Forrester Research. Below are some of the important things to keep in mind before creating a CoP.

- Clear purpose – What is the vision for the CoP?

- Creating a trusted and effective environment for knowledge sharing and collaboration

- Committed core group of active participants

- CoP members motivated to contribute to initiatives

- Knowing the needs of participants

- Having a clear action plan with activities to meet needs

- Blending face-to-face and online activities

Tools will be introduced at various phases to the CoP members (Figure 5-16).

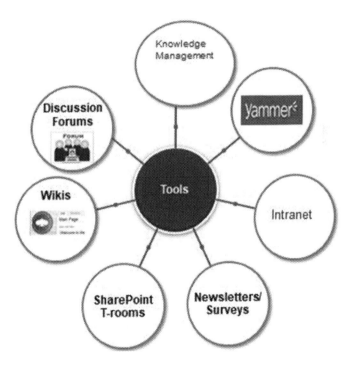

Figure 5-16. *Tools for CoP communities*

Implementation Approach at Various Stages of CoP Building

We will assume this is quarterly:

Q1

1. Create distribution list for CoP members;

2. Create community-space KM portal;

3. Encourage CoP members to join KM2.0 Discussion Forum;

4. Organize monthly meetings for CoP leader to share CoP vision, updates, and plans;

5. Send communications and surveys to CoP members to create awareness and understand interest levels for various planned initiatives.

After the audience, purpose, goals, and vision for the community are identified, we will proceed with the creation of the KM space and the distribution lists for the community. After KM is set up, we can encourage the CoP members to join the KM2 Discussion Forum and start discussions around various CoP topics.

A survey can be rolled out to all the CoP members to help assess if they agree with the CoP model and understand what their expectations from the CoP would be. We can also ask specific questions like if there are any tools or features that they feel would benefit the community. We can use this feedback to create a more tailored CoP model with customized requirements for the CoP.

We can organize monthly webinars for the CoP leader to share the vision, updates, and CoP plans to the community members. This can be a one-hour webinar with a 40-minute presentation and 20 minutes for Q&A.

Q2

1. Create Yammer community and invite CoP members to join;

2. Launch webcast series on topics to be presented by SMEs within CoP;

3. Promote CoP specific University learning courses to community members;

4. Send communication flyers on Learning and Development courses and webcasts to CoP members.

Here are some notes on the process:

- A Yammer Community can be created for the CoP to increase collaboration and networking between the community members.

- A webcast series can be launched on hot topics presented by SMEs within the CoP. These webcasts can be delivered with the help of the Our University team on the Adobe Connect platform. The webcasts can be highly interactive with the usage of Adobe Connect tools like polling questions, white board, chat pod, etc.

- We can work with Our University to promote CoP-specific university learning courses to the community members. Mailers can be sent on a quarterly basis to the CoP members with the list of available trainings from learning and development teams.

Q3

1. Send Newsletter on CoP updates and events.

2. Plan Face-to-face meetings for focused meetings on special topics.

3. Plan CoP specific training events with the help of Learning and Development teams.

4. Newsletters/Newsflashes can be sent on a quarterly/ bimonthly basis to keep the community members updated on the latest CoP news and initiatives.

Some notes on this stage:

- Newsletters would have interactive features like surveys and opinion polls to gather feedback from the CoP members on various initiatives.

- SPOCs within the CoP can help facilitate Face-to-Face regional meetings on focused topics. Frequency of the meetings would depend on the interest level of the groups.

- CoP-specific training events can be organized with help of Our University on a quarterly basis. These trainings can be presented by SMEs within the CoP and also moderated by CoP members.

Q4

1. Study KM portal usage and plan revamp of pages accordingly.

2. Introduce a best practice sharing campaign:

- CoP members can contribute ideas and also comment and discuss posted ideas.

- Top idea contributors should be recognized.

Finally, some notes on this stage:

- Recognition – Promote quality contributors on a quarterly basis on KM2.0 and Newsletters and also ensure that you spotlight valuable CoP contributions.

- A best practice sharing campaign can be introduced for CoP members to share their best practices and ideas. Other CoP members can comment and discuss the posted ideas to make it interactive. Top contributors can be recognized with some prizes.

- Community KM2.0 usage analytics can be studied for performing site audit on a half-yearly basis. Portal revamp can also be planned based on feedback from CoP members.

Summary

With this, we have come to the end of the chapter. In this chapter, we have taken a deep into a SharePoint-based system such as Solution Database; Ask the Expert; and a cursory overview for Communities of Practices, which will help to execute KM initiatives in a collaborative way using SharePoint Online technology. In the next chapter, we will focus on the use of Artificial Intelligence in strengthening CX.

CHAPTER 6

AI in DCX

Now that we have come to the last chapter of this book, we will spend
some time looking at how artificial intelligence (AI) has created a big
impact on digital customer experience (DCX). But before going into it, let's
recapitulate things we have learned up to now. At the start of the book, we
started exploring SharePoint Online features and Office 365 tools, which
help to build DCX experience, and we concluded that technology is an
enabler to create DCX. We saw a couple of applications built-in SharePoint
Online such as a Solution Database used in the Incident Management
process and Communities of Practice, which help like-minded community
members collaborate faster. Later, we took a deep dive into CX and
DCX and discovered various ways to create DCX Finally, in the previous
chapter we saw that a new Software Development Life Cycle involves a
User Experience and User Interface process built in it; and finally, we saw
hands-on UI assessment of an application built in SharePoint Online.

In this final chapter, we will look how AI has impacted DCX. Infusing
AI into digital customer platforms makes CX more human and at a
scale previously unimaginable – it's improving the quality of life for the
individual customer and employee and thus boosting DCX. SharePoint
Online is an SaaS and has inline AI. We will see a lot of AI, which will
hopefully inspire you to create a custom solution by integrating AI
technology with SharePoint Online. Let's see the impact of AI:

- An exponential volume of exploitable data that results
  in more and more accurate AI systems

© Charles Waghmare 2020
C. Waghmare, *Augmenting Customer Experience with SharePoint Online*,
https://doi.org/10.1007/978-1-4842-5534-6_6

- Improved scalability and elasticity at lower costs through cloud computing

- Complex deep learning through processing hardware breakthroughs

- Increasingly comprehensive AI due to new technology such as machine language, machine learning, and deep learning algorithms

Current State of AI

Figure 6-1 represents some AI technology that is currently available.

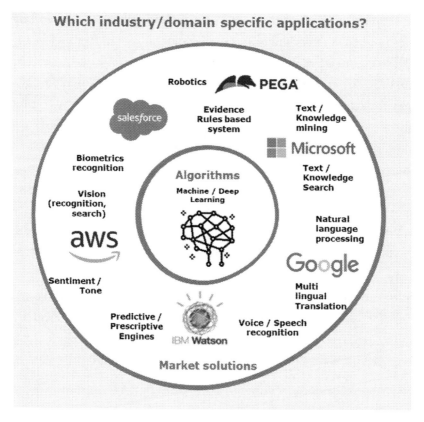

Figure 6-1. *Industry domain-specific AI applications*

Here are some more details:

- Google is using natural language processing (NLP) and multilingual translation for processing information coming in as input from the end user.

- Microsoft uses text knowledge mining and text knowledge search for dealing with content and search aspects respectively.

- IBM Watson has speech recognition and predictive/ prescriptive engines that transforms input received in the form voice, processes it, searches within the database, and gives an answer in the form of voice.

- Amazon Web Services has a sentiment tone to capture tone/sentiment of conversation and vision recognition AIs.

- Salesforce has a robotic process automation tool called UiPath and biometric recognition.

- Finally, a business process management (BPM) tool called PEGA has an evidence rules-based system to make decisions.

Evolution of AI

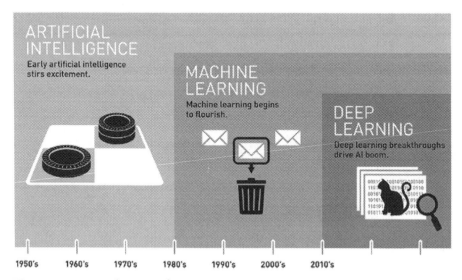

Figure 6-2. *Evolution of AI*

- As seen in Figure 6-2: 1950s to 1980s: Set of technologies developed with the goal of reproducing certain human-specific tasks.

- As seen in Figure 6-2: 1980s to 2010s: Subfield of computer science that "gives computers the ability to learn without being explicitly programmed."

- As seen in Figure 6-2: 2010s onward: Subset of machine learning that has networks that can learn unsupervised from data that is unstructured or unlabeled.

In 2018, a survey conducted on 1000 adults in the United Kingdom on AI revealed these interesting facts:

- Lack of knowledge: only 1/10 know about AI

- 60% of respondents believed AI represented a lack of job security for people

- 48% believed machines or technology will make bad choices

- 42% expressed discomfort interacting with chatbots

- 53% heard of having a cybersecurity attack

- 52% of respondents said they were worried about less security of personal data and privacy

- 89% said AI will make complex jobs easier

- Top 5 perceived benefits of AI-based Robots:

  - Advances in medicine 54%

  - Increased production 40%

  - Increased industry standards 39%

  - Increased space travel 38%

  - Increasing quality of life 34%

This survey shows that AI was still immature until last year; however, with an increased demand for competition and CX, investment in AI has grown exponentially. One of the largest market research companies, Gartner, predicted that investment in AI has been growing exponentially since the last couple of years and is expected to rise form the current $2.1 billion to $36.1 billion in 2025 – just in the health-care sector.

Benefits of AI

A large French IT services company, Capgemini, performed a digital transformation study. It appears AI is becoming the best tool to reach and engage customers while boosting efficiency. A result appeared, showing that the share of firms implementing AI observed a more than 10% benefit compared to those areas where there was no AI.

Post AI implementation by some organizations saw benefits in false positive reduction, higher compliance at lower cost, reduction in operational cost, increase in employee's productivity, and increased operational efficiency. Figure 6-3 shows the percentage growth in these mentioned areas.

Figure 6-3. *Benefits post AI implementation*

Figure 6-4 shows the share of organizations implementing AI that observe more than a 10%-point gain in the area of churn reduction, reduced customer complaints, and enhanced customer satisfaction.

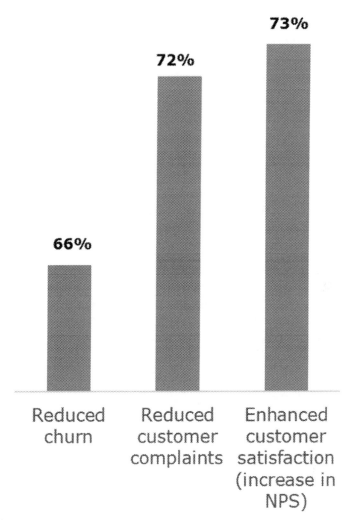

Figure 6-4. *Critical growth areas post AI implementation*

Estimated benefits when investing in AI are found to be increasing response rates, reducing retention discounts, finding incremental sales opportunities, reducing churn rates, increasing NPS, reducing contact center communications, reducing processing times, and increasing conversion rates (all shown in Figure 6-5).

Increasing response rate

Reducing retention discounts

Finding incremental sales opportunities

Reducing churn rates

Increasing NPS

Reducing contact center communications

Reducing processing time

Increasing conversion rate

Figure 6-5. *Estimated Benefits*

AI Intelligent System Boosting Sales

In Figure 6-6, AI allows companies to personalize users' experiences by enabling them to scale up human connection and engagement. AI simplifies and personalizes user experience with natural language-based conversations that will progressively become the vehicle of choice for connecting individual consumers with brands. AI relieves employees from repetitive tasks (automation) and feeds them with predictions / recommendations (augmentation) for a better focus on judgment / decision when engaging and serving customers, at scale.

In Figure 6-6, a conversation with brands takes place with humans and technology working together. A typical customer has qualities such as simplicity in giving clear commands and that too in real time, who built trust with brand, being proactive and creating personal conversational. Dialogue between a customer and AI system drives loyalty. Humans and technology go hand-in-hand to be scalable, achieve growth and efficiency, and decide or predict customer inputs. This improves efficiency. Intelligent applications based on AI combine brand conversations with human and technology working together in order to boost sales. Brand conversations lead to a customer-centric focus, buying pattern, attention to precise requirements, infuses offers based on customer personas, and seasonal patterns help in boosting sales.

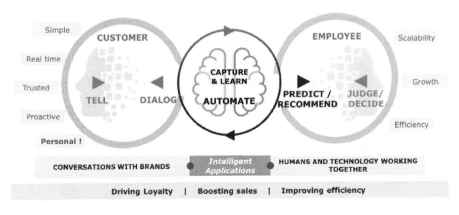

Figure 6-6. *AI Intelligence application boosting sales*

AI Application Domains

The four intelligent applications enabled by infusing AI into CX to achieve customer goals and enterprise goals are customer understanding, immersive experience, conversational interfaces, and employee augmentation (Figure 6-7).

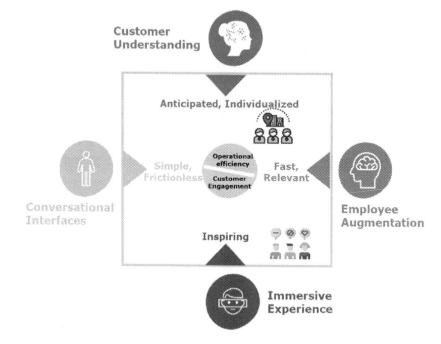

Figure 6-7. *Enabled by infusing AI into CX*

Customer Understanding

This involves a continuous effort to capture, process, and analyze customers' data in real time from interactions, journeys, events, and emotions in order to build a holistic view of the customer as well as an actionable insight of its needs, expectations, and brand empathy.

Below are different types of AI in DCX use cases:

- Customer empathy

- Customer social personality

- Customer propensities and scoring

- Customer journey patterns

- Brand sentiment and reputation

- Analyze audience, journey, and interactions

- Enrich data (behavioral, emotional, and images related)

- Segment and cluster

- Detect churn

Employee Augmentation

This features augmenting the employee in decision-making and unstructured data analysis and improving their focus on customer-facing activities with more efficiency, reactivity, and relevance.

Below are different types of AI in DCX use cases:

- Marketing:

    - Market watch

    - Engagement scoring

    - Audiences segmentations

    - Dynamic re-targeting

    - Next best message

    - Personalized content

- Sales:

    - Account insights

    - Lead and opportunity scoring

    - Dynamic pricing

    - Sales coaching and advising

    - Forecasting

    - X/Upsell – next best offer

- Services:

    - Contacts qualification and distribution

    - Field service augmentation

    - Knowledge of customer service

    - Anti-churn recommendations

- Commerce:

    - Product recommendations

    - Predictive search

    - Dynamic pricing

Immersive Experience

This is a combination of vision, voice, and natural language AI techniques with immersive applications (augmented, virtual, and mixed reality) aiming at enriching user experience and interactions with products and services, all along the customer life cycle.

Below are different types of AI in DCX use cases:

- Facial recognition / analysis

- Image recognition for augmented product experience

- Use facial recognition (ex., for payment)

- Use image recognition for augmented product experience

- Provide voice assistants for purchase

- Analyze emotions in-store

- Analyze traffic in-store

Conversational Interfaces

This is a combination of chat, voice, vision, or any other natural language interface aiming at transforming user interactions into human conversations.

Below are different types of AI in DCX use cases:

- Conversations with customers

- Assistants for employees

- Questions and answers

- Capture the customer dialogue

- Understand the written and spoken language

- Monitor quality dialogue

- Automate customer service

Monitor Business Impacts of AI in DCX

To monitor business impacts of AI in DCX, there are parameters that can be considered to improve CX improve efficiency, optimize costs, and increase revenue. We will see each of the categories in detail, in order to measure the business value of AI (Figure 6-8).

	Customer understanding	Employee augmentation	Conversational interfaces	Immersive experience
Improve customer experience — Customer retention	X	X		
Customer satisfaction	X	X	X	X
Customer engagement (NPS)	X	X	X	X
Seamless Customer Experience (effort score, drop out rate)			X	X
First call resolution	X	X	X	
Improve efficiency & optimize costs — Product marketing (Time to Market for launching new offering)	X	X		X
Employee productivity/efficiency		X		
Average handle time (AHT)	X	X	X	
Employee satisfaction		X	X	
Deflection (use of digital channels, vocal assistants…)			X	
Increase revenue — Forecast accuracy	X	X		
Marketing efficiency	X	X		
Upsell/cross sell (average basket)	X	X		X
Lead conversion rate		X		

Figure 6-8. *Measure AI business value impact with focused success metrics*

Below are some important areas around which we can measure the business value of AI.

Customer Satisfaction

- Request understanding (FCR: First Call Resolution), voice synthesis quality

- Share in fully automated interactions for the selected use case

- Transfer rate to an advisor (triggered by a client's request / misunderstanding)

- Conversion rate / additional sales

- Customer satisfaction (NPS: Net Promoter Score is a metric for assessing customer loyalty)

Technical

- A bot's ability to replicate a human task, for example, text mining

- Bot's response time (latency)

- Failure rate during personalized information collection

- Data reliability / accuracy

- Failure rate during the transfer to an advisor

- Scalability rate

- Execution time reduction

Employees

- Advisor satisfaction (periodic survey)

- Focus on added value tasks

- Work conditions

Operational

- Intention recognition rate

- Speech to text (STT) recognition rate

- Average interaction duration:

  - Interaction with the bot

  - Interaction with the advisor

- Post-call treatment time

- Average waiting time duration

- Share of automated tasks

AI for CX Client Stories

A cruise line wants to deliver a differentiated CX for the millennial travelers. So, they adopted the following systems:

- Facial recognition for frictionless boarding experience

- Entertainment survey with emotion recognition and audience analytics

- Predictive analytics for customer segmentation and dynamically optimized recommendations

- Social media mining with NLP and sentiment analysis

- Fuse various third-party data sources to cluster prospective voyagers

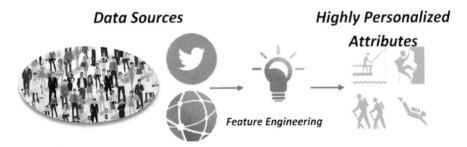

Figure 6-9. *Data sources to cluster prospective voyagers*

An automotive OEM delivers DCX for their test-drive experience to improve a lead qualification.

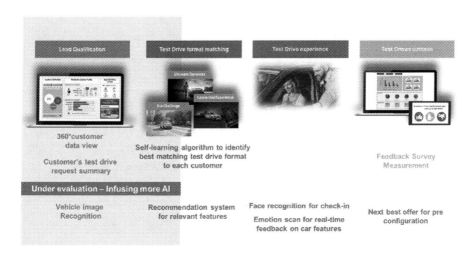

Figure 6-10. *Success story AI in CX*

A leading entertainment company wants to drive their restaurants'
sales up.

Figure 6-11. *Success story AI in CX*

Scope for Compliance AI in DCX

Scope for compliance falls into transparent, accountable, and ethical categories.

Transparent

- Reassure the customer
- Inform about GDPR rights (rights to be informed, to have access to information, to be forgotten...)
- Implement consent forms
- Specify the contact person
- Accuracy

Accountable

- Comply to regulations
- Define responsibility in legal contracts
- Appoint a data protection officer (DPO)
- Rely on accountable algorithms and processes (information access, encryption, use, transfer (...) and scheduled deletion)
- Implement cybersecurity tools and traceability processes and controls
- Use EU-approved data centers
- Explicability

Ethical

- Maximize efficiency while ensuring ethics
- Ensure the consumer's privacy
- Provide bias-free bots

Future Considerations

Anticipating future regulation compliance and ethical requirements involves the following:

- Loss of control (self-driving cars, smart house tools, discrimination/bias...)

- Lack of transparency (who/what is behind the screen - bots impersonating)

- Absence of algorithm traceability and explicability (e.g., neural networks) / fake data

- Unsecured access to information (leaks, fraud...)

- Misuse of confidential information (social anxiety, consent bypass)

- Failure to perform (who is responsible in case of damage?)

- R&D (research and development) deviations such as in clinical trials to detect potential protocol deviations, such as the emergence of a non-random variation trend

Best Practices for Creating an AI-Infused DCX Road Map

These nine best practices fall into empowering clients to deliver new customer-centric business models, transforming them toward humanized customer experiences, and experimenting with a new technology and architecture focus.

Empowering clients to deliver new customer-centric business models:

- Design and deliver AI-first customer platforms at scale to support newer business models

- Continuously revisit and apply AI innovations to adapt services and products portfolio

- Continuously learn from and connect with customers' behaviors and emotions to adapt business models

Transforming toward humanized customer experiences:

- Amplify existing user experiences with natural language (voice, text) and vision. Experiment with customer emotions hidden in customer conversations, to predict insights

- Implement predictive solutions for next best action and connect them with user experiences

- Deliver and connect the customer data architecture that enables customer platforms to learn and predict

Experimenting a new technology and architecture focus:

- Evaluate AI technologies and their applications for CX, understand their potential and limits

- Experiment use cases for CX by infusing AI technology, platforms, tools, and solutions

- Enable the organization to continuously experiment and infuse AI into CX

Summary

In this chapter, we have taken a deep dive into AI pertaining to customer experience. We saw how intelligent systems linked with AI to produce DCX. SharePoint Online can also be integrated with AI tools that we have discovered in order to create DCX. AI in CX will take a long leap in the coming years as companies are investing in AI to bring DCX.

Index

V

Vision API, 55

W, X

Webparts, 21–23

Y, Z

Yammer, 33
Yammer webpart, 35
    conversations, 35
    post message, 36
    Yammer group URL, 36

Printed in the United States
By Bookmasters